ANIMAL
Origami

ARCTURUS

ARCTURUS

This edition published in 2016 by Arcturus Publishing Limited
26/27 Bickels Yard, 151–153 Bermondsey Street,
London SE1 3HA

Models and photography by Belinda Webster and Michael Wiles
Written by Joe Fullman
Designed by Amy McSimpson
Edited by Frances Evans
Cartoon elements from Shutterstock

ISBN: 978-1-78428-212-7
CH004933NT
Supplier 26, Date 0716, Print run 5237

Printed in China

Contents

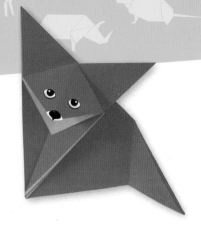

Introduction

This book shows you how to make an incredible menagerie of paper animals and create your own really wild scenes!

In traditional origami, models are made from one sheet of folded paper and there is no cutting involved. We've broken the rules a little, to give the animals legs, snouts, and other features. Ask an adult to help with any projects that need scissors. Otherwise, all you need to get started is a square of paper, your fingers, and some simple folds.

Getting Started

The paper used in origami is thin but strong, so that it can be folded many times. You can use ordinary scrap paper, as long as it's not too thick.

A lot of the origami models in this book are made with the same folds. This introduction explains some of the ones that will appear most, so it's a good idea to master these folds before you start. When making the projects, follow the key below to find out what the lines and arrows mean. And always crease well!

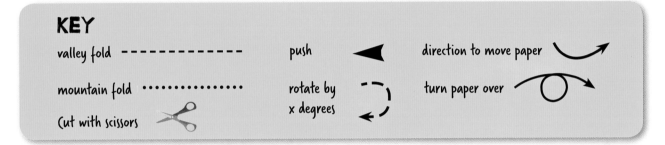

KEY

valley fold ------------

mountain fold ●●●●●●●●●●●●

Cut with scissors ✂

push ◀

rotate by x degrees ⟲

direction to move paper ↘

turn paper over ↻

MOUNTAIN FOLD

To make a mountain fold, fold the paper so that the crease is pointing up toward you, like a mountain.

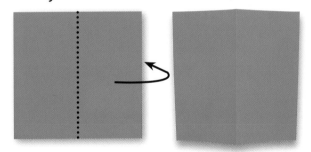

VALLEY FOLD

To make a valley fold, fold the paper the other way, so that the crease is pointing away from you, like a valley.

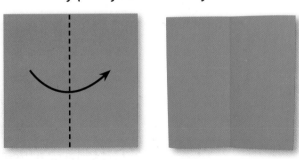

STEP FOLD

A step fold is used to make a step or zigzag in the paper. We'll use it to make ears, tails, and other animal features.

1 Valley fold the paper in half. Then make a mountain fold directly above the valley fold.

2 Push the mountain fold over the valley fold and press down flat.

3 You now have a step fold. You can also make it in reverse, with the mountain fold first.

INSIDE REVERSE FOLD

This is useful if you want to flatten part of an origami model. It's a good way to create tails and noses for your animals.

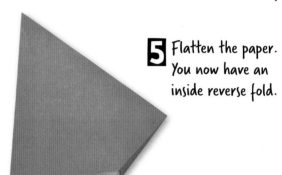

1 Fold a piece of paper diagonally in half. Make a valley fold on one point and crease.

2 It's important to make sure that the paper is creased well. Run your finger over the crease two or three times.

3 Unfold and open up the corner slightly. Refold the crease you just made into a mountain fold.

Open

4 Open up the paper a little more and then tuck the tip of the point inside. Close the paper. This is the view from the underside of the paper.

5 Flatten the paper. You now have an inside reverse fold.

OUTSIDE REVERSE FOLD

This is great if you want to make part of your model stick out. It will come in handy for making paws and ears.

1 Fold a piece of paper diagonally in half. Make a valley fold on one point and crease.

2 It's important to make sure that the paper is creased well. Run your finger over the crease two or three times.

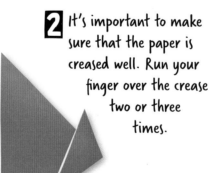

3 Unfold and open up the corner slightly. Refold the crease you just made into a mountain fold.

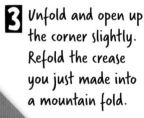

Open

4 Open up the paper a little more and start to turn the corner inside out. Then close the paper when the fold begins to turn.

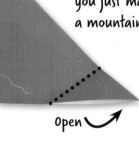

5 You now have an outside reverse fold. You can either flatten the paper or leave it rounded out.

On Safari

Take a trip to the African savannah with these incredible safari animals!

Lion

ROAR!

Monkey

Elephant

Giraffe

Rhino

CHARGE!

Elephant

Elephants are the largest animals on land. Here's how to fold a little, paper version!

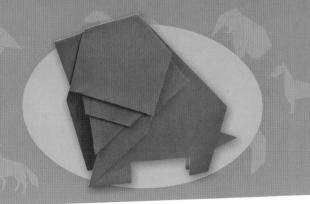

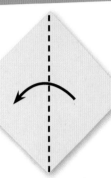

1 Place your paper white side up with a corner facing you. Valley fold it in half from right to left, then unfold.

2 Make a diagonal fold a third of the way between the top left edge and the central crease.

3 Repeat step 2 on the right-hand side.

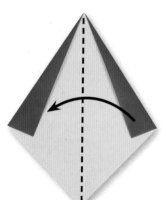

4 Fold the paper in half from right to left.

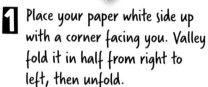
45°

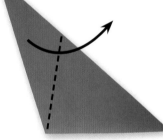

5 Rotate your paper 45° to the left, so the short straight edge is facing you.

6 Fold the top left point over to the right, like this.

Open

7 Open out the pocket you made in step 6.

Push

8 As you open out the folds from step 6, push down the top point and flatten down the paper.

9 Your paper should look like this. Make two small cuts along the solid lines. Mountain fold the paper behind on either side.

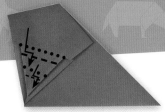

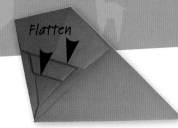

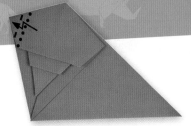

10 Make two step folds (see page 5), as shown, to form the elephant's trunk.

11 Your paper should look like this. Flatten the folds down.

12 Make a step fold on the left-hand side, as shown, to form the first ear.

13 Repeat step 12 on the other side.

14 Begin making the tail by valley folding the right-hand point back to the left. Fold it the other way so it's also a mountain fold.

15 Make another valley fold, slightly to the right of the one you made in step 14. Again, fold it the other way so it's also a mountain fold.

16 Now turn the folds you made in steps 14 and 15 into two inside reverse folds (see page 6), one inside the other to finish the tail.

18

Draw in the eyes and your elephant is ready! Remember, elephants live in family groups, so why not make him some brothers and sisters?

17 Your paper should look like this. Use your scissors to cut out a small rectangle to make your elephant's legs.

Giraffe

A giraffe's long neck helps it to reach the tastiest leaves right at the tops of trees.

1 Place your paper white side up with a corner facing you. Valley fold it in half from right to left, then unfold.

2 Valley fold the right corner to the central crease, as shown.

3 Repeat step 2 on the left-hand side.

4 Fold the paper in half from right to left.

45°

5 Your paper should look like this. Rotate it 45° so the short flat side faces you.

6 Make a valley fold in the position shown.

Fold over

9 Make a valley fold, as shown, to begin the head.

7 Fold it the other way, so it's also a mountain fold.

8 Turn the folds you made in steps 6 and 7 into an outside reverse fold (see page 6).

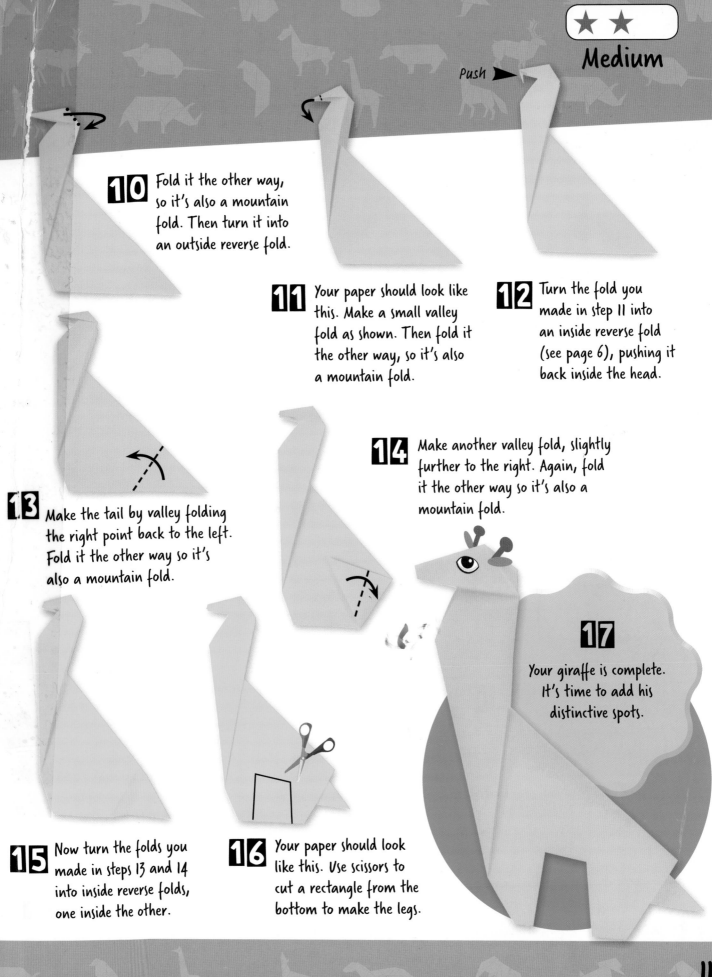

Push ▶

10 Fold it the other way, so it's also a mountain fold. Then turn it into an outside reverse fold.

11 Your paper should look like this. Make a small valley fold as shown. Then fold it the other way, so it's also a mountain fold.

12 Turn the fold you made in step 11 into an inside reverse fold (see page 6), pushing it back inside the head.

13 Make the tail by valley folding the right point back to the left. Fold it the other way so it's also a mountain fold.

14 Make another valley fold, slightly further to the right. Again, fold it the other way so it's also a mountain fold.

17 Your giraffe is complete. It's time to add his distinctive spots.

15 Now turn the folds you made in steps 13 and 14 into inside reverse folds, one inside the other.

16 Your paper should look like this. Use scissors to cut a rectangle from the bottom to make the legs.

Lion

Follow these steps to create your own king of the beasts with a magnificent mane!

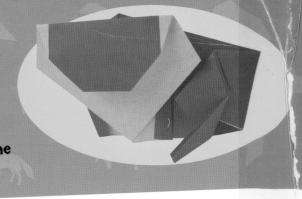

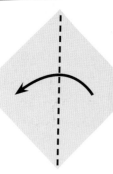

1 Place your paper white side up with a corner facing you. Valley fold it in half from right to left, then unfold.

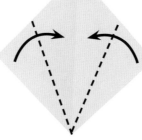

2 Fold the left and right bottom edges to the central crease.

3 Make two small mountain folds at the top of the central flaps.

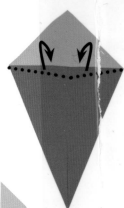

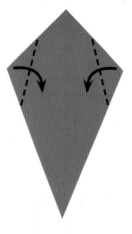

4 Your paper should look like this. Turn it over from left to right.

5 Make two small valley folds on the left and right sides.

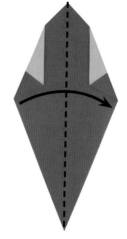

6 Valley fold the paper in half from left to right.

7 Your paper should look like this. Rotate it 90° to the left.

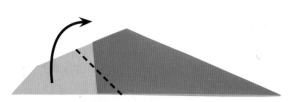

8 Fold the left corner up and to the right, as shown.

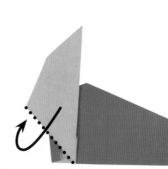

9 Fold it back on itself so it's also a mountain fold, then turn it into an inside reverse fold (see page 6).

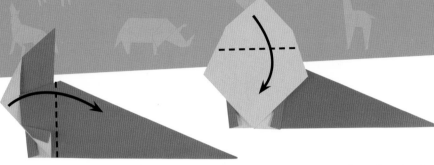

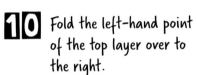

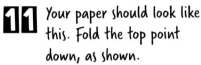

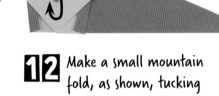

10 Fold the left-hand point of the top layer over to the right.

11 Your paper should look like this. Fold the top point down, as shown.

12 Make a small mountain fold, as shown, tucking the point behind.

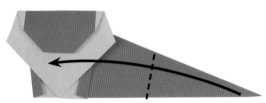

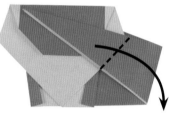

13 Fold the right hand point up and over to the left.

14 Now fold it down and to the right.

15 Make a third fold, taking it back over to the left.

18

Add eyes, nose, whiskers, and a mouth, and your lion is ready to roar.

16 Make a final fourth fold back to the right, then turn this into an inside reverse fold.

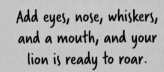

Pull

17 Your paper should look like this. Gently pull the tail out to help your lion stand.

13

Rhino

The word "rhinoceros" means "nose horn". Crease your paper well to make sure your rhino's horn is extra strong.

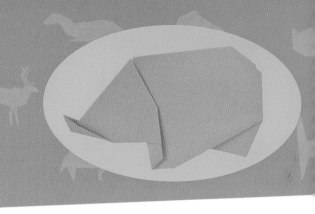

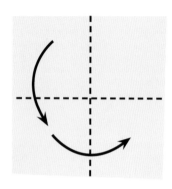

1 Place your paper white side up with a straight edge facing you. Valley fold it in half from top to bottom, and unfold. Then valley fold it in half from left to right, and unfold.

2 Fold the top left corner down to the central point.

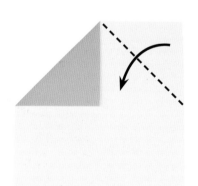

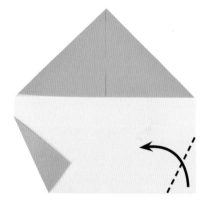

4 Make a small valley fold in the bottom left corner, as shown.

3 Repeat step 2 on the right-hand side.

5 Repeat step 4 on the right-hand side.

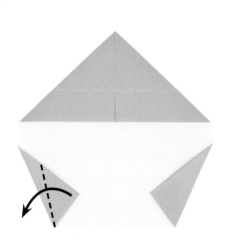

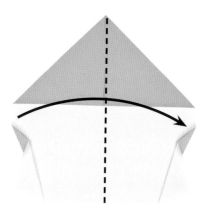

7 Repeat step 6 on the right-hand side.

6 Valley fold the flap you made in step 4 back to the left, as shown.

8 Your paper should look like this. Valley fold it in half from left to right.

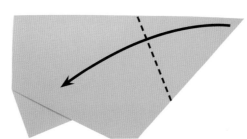

90°

10 Valley fold the right-hand point over to the left.

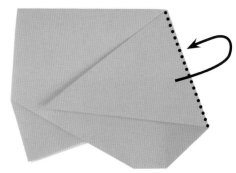

9 Rotate your paper 90° to the right, so the long straight edge is at the top.

11 Fold it back to the right so it's also a mountain fold.

Rhino... continued

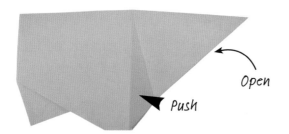

Open

Push

12 Open up the right-hand point slightly and push it back to the left.

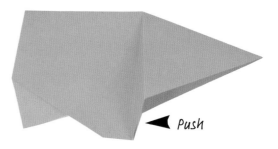

Push

13 Keep pushing, so that the folds you made in steps 10 and 11 go either side of the main bit of paper.

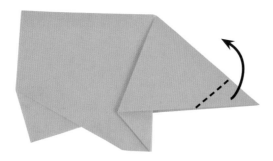

14 Your paper should look like this. Fold the right-hand point up a little way.

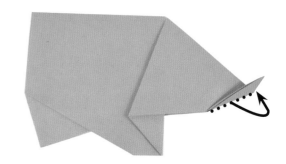

15 Fold it back the other way so it's also a mountain fold.

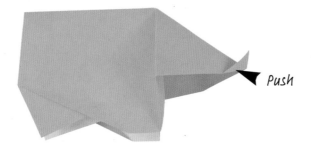

Push

16 Turn the fold inside out and push it back on itself to form an outside reverse fold (see page 6). This is the horn.

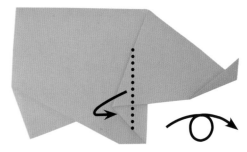

17 Make a small mountain fold, as shown. Then turn the paper over.

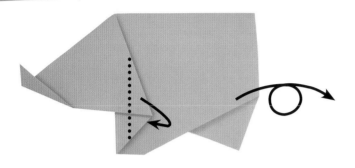

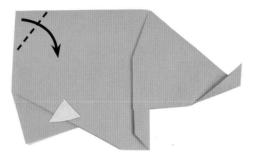

18 Repeat step 17 on the other side, then turn the paper back over.

19 Make a small valley fold in the top left corner.

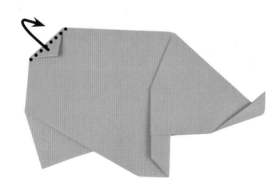

20 Fold it the other way, so it's also a mountain fold then turn it into an inside reverse fold (see page 6).

21

Time for your rhinoceros to make its first charge.

Monkey

Follow these steps to fold a funny paper monkey.
You can hang him up wherever you like!

1 Place your paper white side up with a straight edge facing you. Valley fold it in half from top to bottom, and unfold. Then valley fold it in half from left to right, and unfold.

2 Turn the paper over, so that the orange side is facing up. Diagonally valley fold it one way, and unfold. Then diagonally valley fold it the other way, and unfold.

Push ◄   Push ◄

3 Turn the paper over again, so the white side is facing up, and rotate it so a corner is facing you. Then start pushing the two outer corners in to meet each other.

Flatten

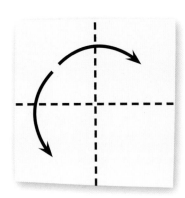

4 As you push, the paper should start folding up into a small square like this. Flatten it down.

5 Your paper should look like this. Valley fold the left bottom edge of the top layer over to the central line.

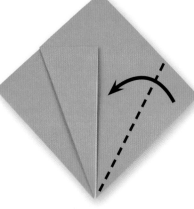

6 Valley fold the right bottom edge of the top layer over to the central line.

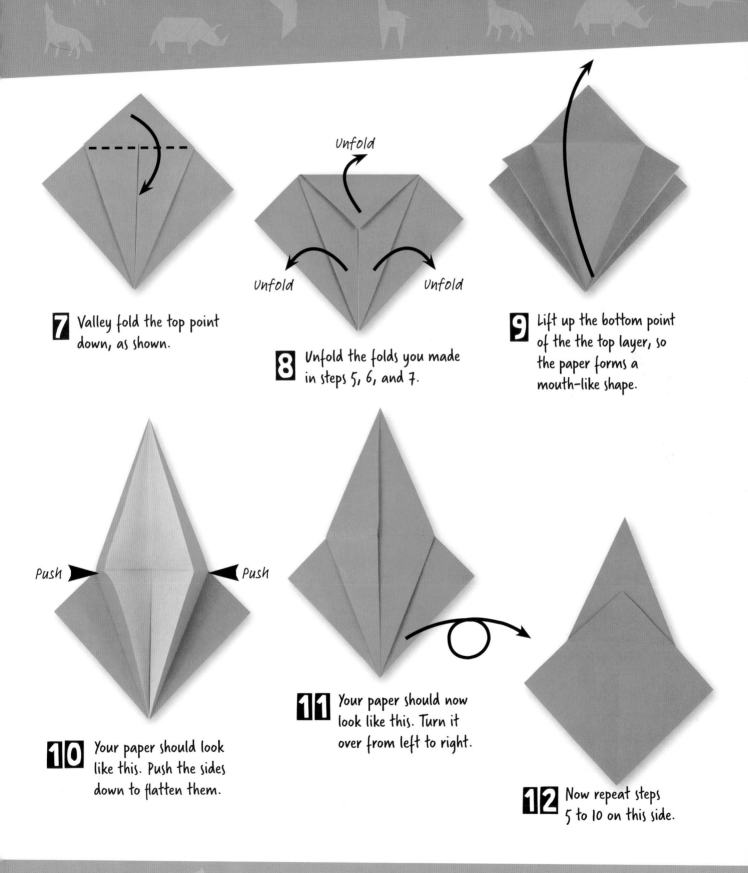

7 Valley fold the top point down, as shown.

8 Unfold the folds you made in steps 5, 6, and 7.

Unfold

Unfold

Unfold

9 Lift up the bottom point of the the top layer, so the paper forms a mouth-like shape.

Push ◄   ► Push

10 Your paper should look like this. Push the sides down to flatten them.

11 Your paper should now look like this. Turn it over from left to right.

12 Now repeat steps 5 to 10 on this side.

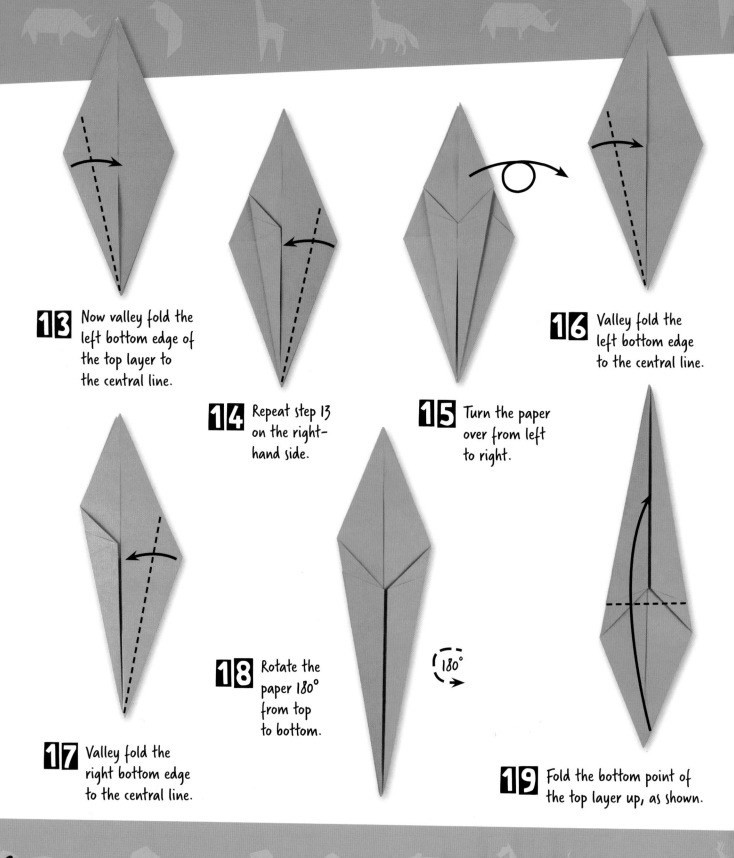

13 Now valley fold the left bottom edge of the top layer to the central line.

14 Repeat step 13 on the right-hand side.

15 Turn the paper over from left to right.

16 Valley fold the left bottom edge to the central line.

17 Valley fold the right bottom edge to the central line.

18 Rotate the paper 180° from top to bottom.

180°

19 Fold the bottom point of the top layer up, as shown.

20

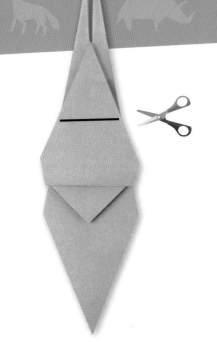

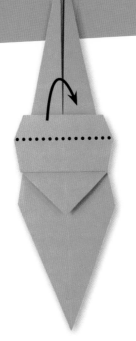

20 Cut across the top layer, as shown, using a pair of scissors.

21 Mountain fold over the cut edge of the paper, as shown.

22 Make a small step fold (see page 5).

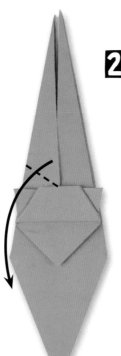

24 Make a valley fold, then fold it the other way, so it's also a mountain fold. Then, using just the two top layers, turn it into an outside reverse fold (see page 6).

23 Repeat step 22 on the other side.

25 Make a valley fold to form the first hand.

Monkey... continued

26 Use scissors to cut a line up the middle, as shown.

27 Make a mountain fold to form the first foot.

28 Make a mountain fold to form the other foot.

31

Your monkey is ready. Be sure to give him a funny expression.

29 Make a valley fold to form the second hand.

30 Make a mountain fold to form the fingers.

Into the Woods

Find out how to fold some cute woodland critters in this chapter.

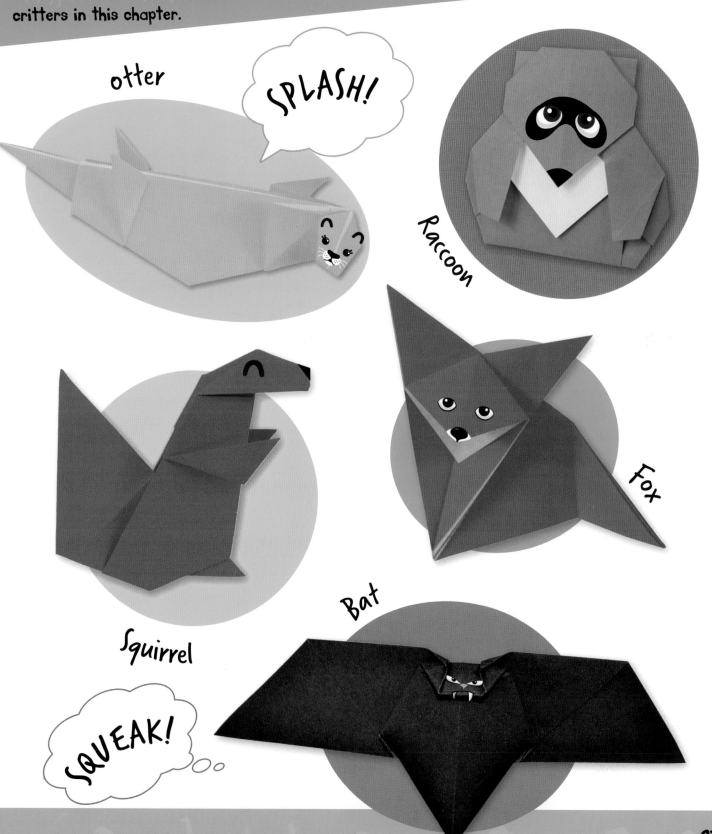

otter

SPLASH!

Raccoon

Squirrel

Fox

Bat

SQUEAK!

Fox

Use red or orange paper to make your own origami fox.

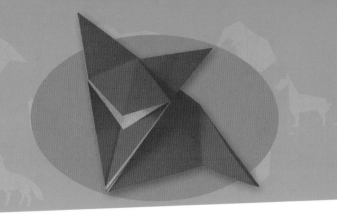

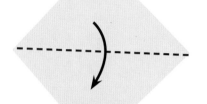

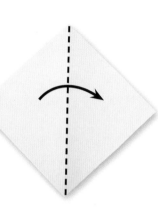

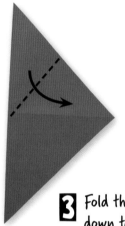

1 Place your paper like this, white side up, with a corner facing you. Valley fold it in half from top to bottom, then unfold.

2 Fold the paper in half from left to right.

3 Fold the top corner down to the right-hand corner.

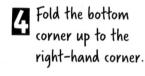

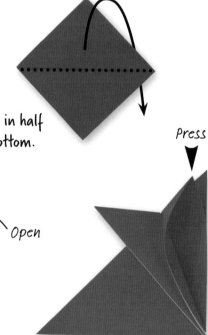

4 Fold the bottom corner up to the right-hand corner.

5 Mountain fold in half from top to bottom.

Press

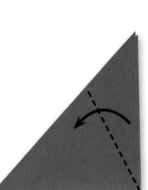

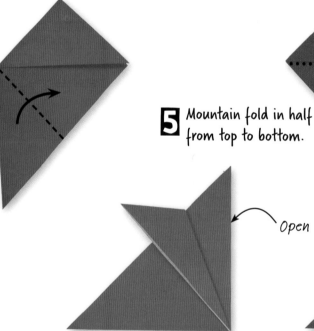

Open

6 Rotate the paper so it looks like this. Fold back the right-hand point of the top layer, as shown.

7 Open up the two layers on the right-hand side so they form a pocket.

8 Press down the top of the pocket and flatten to form the fox's face.

9 Fold the left-hand point to the right to form the tail.

Open

10 Open up the flaps at the bottom of the face to form the mouth.

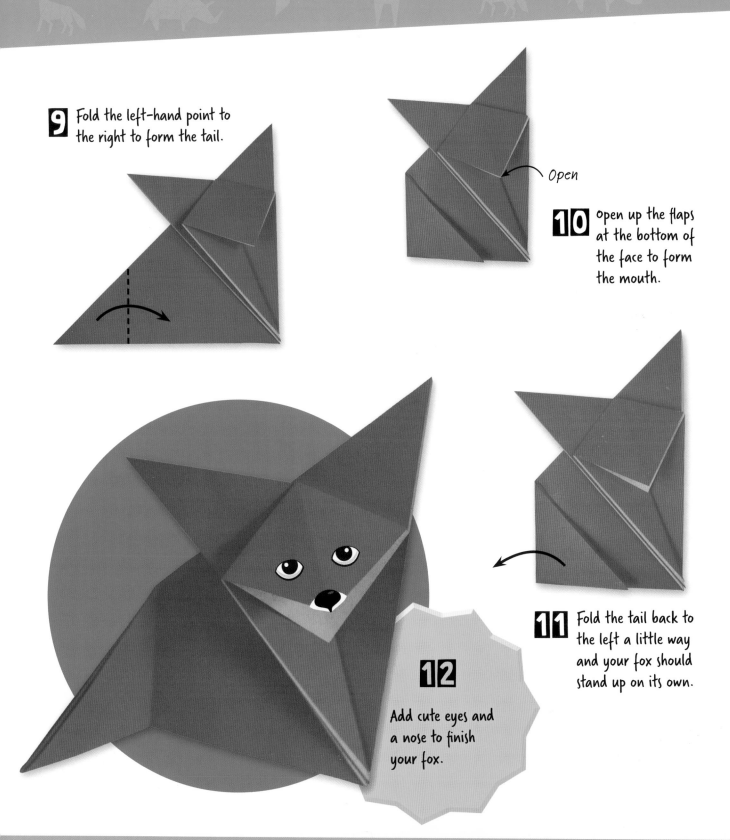

11 Fold the tail back to the left a little way and your fox should stand up on its own.

12

Add cute eyes and a nose to finish your fox.

Bat

Bats are the only mammals that fly. Here's how to make a flapping bat of your own!

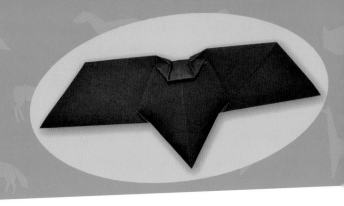

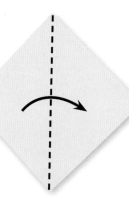

1 Place your paper like this, white side up, with a corner facing you. Valley fold it in half from left to right, then unfold.

2 Fold the paper in half from top to bottom

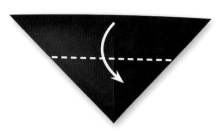

3 Fold the top edge down so it's about ¾ inch (2 cm) from the bottom.

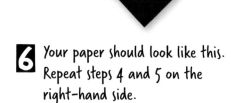

4 Make a diagonal mountain fold, as shown.

5 Make a valley fold ½ inch (1 cm) to the right of the mountain fold to form a step fold (see page 5).

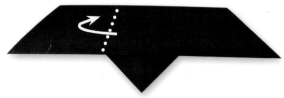

6 Your paper should look like this. Repeat steps 4 and 5 on the right-hand side.

Press   Press

7 Press down the step folds.

8 Make a small valley fold on the left-hand side.

26

9 Make a valley fold on the right.

10 Your paper should look like this. Turn it over from right to left.

11 Make a valley fold at the top, as shown, to form the head.

12 Make a diagonal valley fold to form the first foot.

13 Repeat step 12 on the other side.

14 Add eyes, nose, and a mouth and your bat is complete.

Otter

Otters are playful creatures and love to splash about in the water. Here's how to fold one!

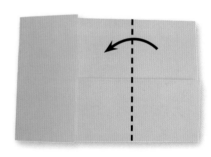

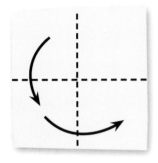

1 With your paper like this, valley fold it in half from top to bottom, and unfold. Then valley fold it in half from left to right, and unfold.

2 Valley fold the top edge down to the central crease.

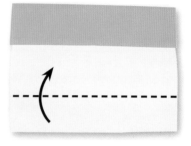

3 Fold the bottom edge up to the central crease.

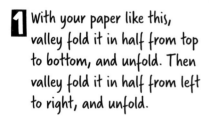

4 Valley fold the left edge to the central crease.

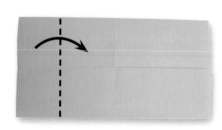

5 Valley fold the right edge to the central crease.

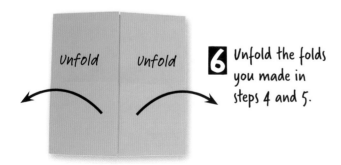

Unfold   Unfold

6 Unfold the folds you made in steps 4 and 5.

7 Fold the top-left corner down to the crease line.

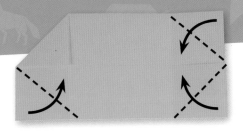

8 Repeat step 7 with the other three corners.

9 Unfold the fold in the top-left corner that you made in step 7.

Open

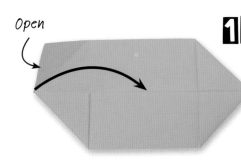

10 Open up the fold and bring its bottom corner over to the right to make a triangle shape.

Flatten

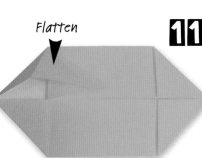

11 Flatten the fold down.

12 Your paper should look like this. Repeat steps 9 to 11 with the other three corners.

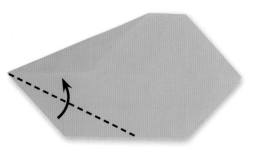

13 Turn the paper over from right to left.

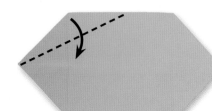

14 Fold the top left corner down to the central crease.

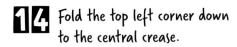

15 Fold the bottom left corner up to the central crease.

29

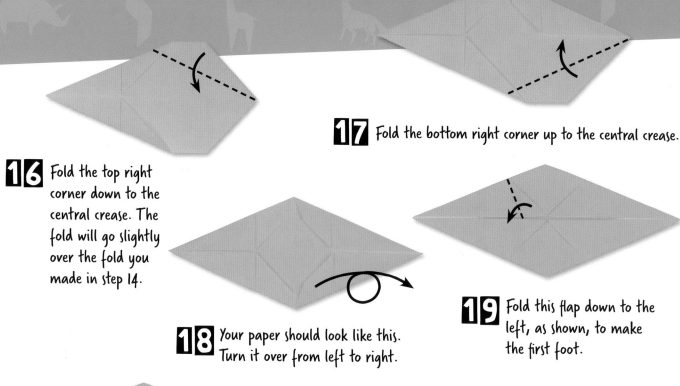

17 Fold the bottom right corner up to the central crease.

16 Fold the top right corner down to the central crease. The fold will go slightly over the fold you made in step 14.

18 Your paper should look like this. Turn it over from left to right.

19 Fold this flap down to the left, as shown, to make the first foot.

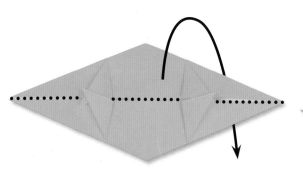

20 Now fold this flap up to the left, so it goes slightly over the flap made in step 19.

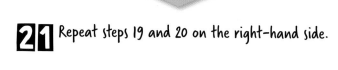

21 Repeat steps 19 and 20 on the right-hand side.

Unfold

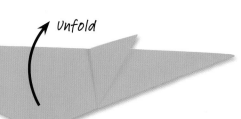

22 Your paper should look like this. Mountain fold it in half from top to bottom.

23 Unfold your paper from bottom to top.

24 Your paper should look like this. Make a step fold on the right-hand side, as shown.

25 Valley fold the paper over from top to bottom.

26 Fold the left-hand point to the right and up, as shown.

27 Make a sharp crease and then fold the point back to the left again.

Push ▶

Open

28 Open up the fold you made in step 27 to form a pocket.

29 Push the left-hand point down and across to make the face.

30 Finally, make a small mountain fold, as shown.

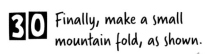

31

Your otter is floating on his back, so be sure to draw his face the right way round.

31

Squirrel

You'll often see a squirrel bouncing about in a forest, collecting tasty nuts and berries to eat.

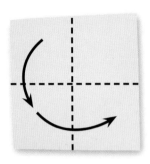

1 With your paper like this, valley fold it in half from top to bottom, and unfold. Then valley fold it in half from left to right, and unfold.

2 Now valley fold the top edge down to the central crease.

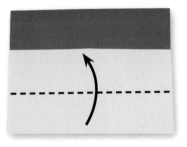

3 Valley fold the bottom edge up to the central crease, too.

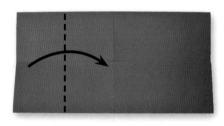

4 Valley fold the left edge to the central crease.

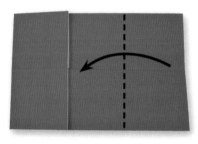

5 Valley fold the right edge to the central crease.

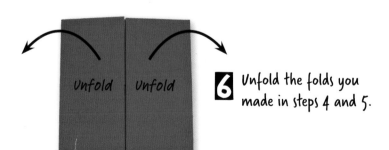

6 Unfold the folds you made in steps 4 and 5.

7 Fold the top-left corner down to the crease line.

32

Hard

8 Repeat step 7 with the other three corners.

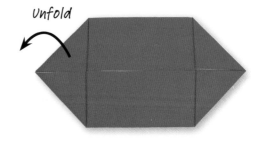

Unfold

9 Unfold the fold in the top-left corner that you made in step 7.

10 Open up the fold and bring its bottom left point over to the right to form a pocket. Then flatten it down to form a triangle shape.

11 Your paper should look like this. Repeat steps 9 and 10 with the other three corners.

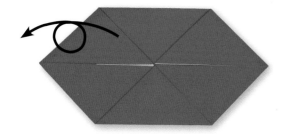

12 Now, your paper should look like this. Turn it over from right to left.

13 Fold the top left corner down to the central crease.

33

14 Fold the bottom left corner up to the central crease.

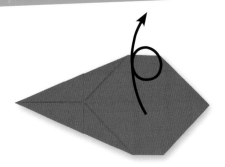

15 Your paper should look like this. Turn it over from bottom to top.

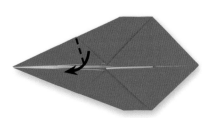

16 Fold this flap down to the left, as shown, to make the first foot.

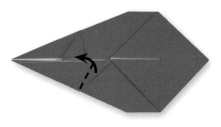

17 Fold up the opposite flap, so it goes slightly over the flap made in step 16.

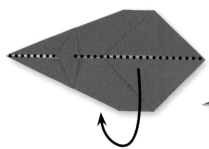

18 Mountain fold the paper in half from bottom to top.

19 Make a diagonal valley fold. Fold it the other way, so it's also a mountain fold, then unfold.

Push

20 Push the right-hand corner up and inside the other folds, pushing along the creases you made in step 19. This will make an inside reverse fold (see page 6).

21 Your paper should look like this. Flatten it down.

22 Rotate your paper 90° to the right.

23 Fold the top point down and to the right, as shown.

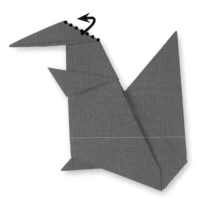

24 Fold it the other way, so it's also a mountain fold, then turn it into an outside reverse fold (see page 6). This is the face.

25 Your paper should look like this. Flatten it down. Make a valley fold at the end of the face. Then fold it the other way, so it's also a mountain fold.

26 Turn the fold you made in step 25 into an inside reverse fold (see page 6), tucking it into the face.

Tuck

27
Your squirrel is ready to collect her first nuts.

Raccoon

Raccoons have stripy tails and black masks on their faces. Give yours some cute markings, too!

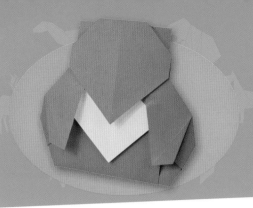

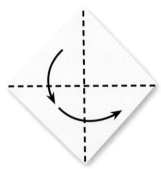

1 With your paper placed like this and white side up, valley fold it in half from top to bottom, and unfold. Then valley fold it in half from left to right, and unfold.

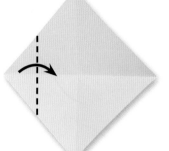

2 Now, valley fold the left corner to the middle crease.

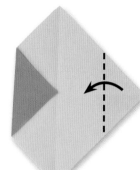

3 Valley fold the right corner to the middle crease.

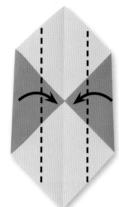

4 Valley fold the left edge and the right edge to the middle so they meet.

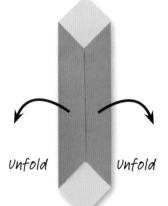

Unfold   Unfold

5 Unfold the folds you made in steps 2 to 4.

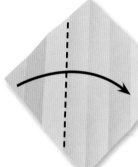

6 Fold the left point so it touches the second crease from the right.

7 Fold back the point at a diagonal angle between the central crease and the crease to its left.

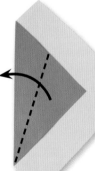

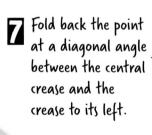

8 Your paper should look like this. Repeat steps 6 and 7 on the right-hand side.

9 Valley fold the bottom point up, as shown.

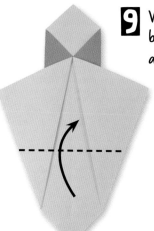

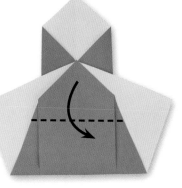

10 Valley fold the top layer down, as shown.

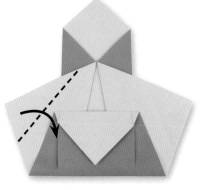

11 Fold the left side across.

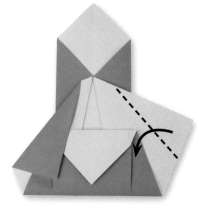

12 Repeat step 11 on the right-hand side.

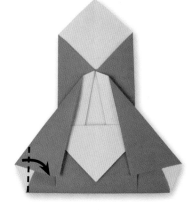

13 Fold over the left-hand point as shown.

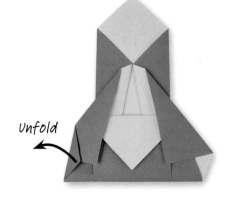

14 Unfold the fold you made in step 13.

Unfold

15 Push the crease of the fold you made in step 13 the other way and behind the flap you made in step 11.

Push

16 Keep pushing and bring the flap you made in step 11 down on top, making a new crease.

Push

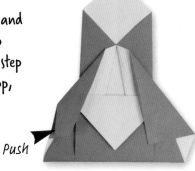

Raccoon... continued

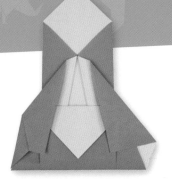

17 Your paper should look like this. Repeat steps 13 to 16 on the right-hand side.

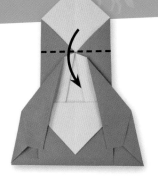

18 Fold the top point down, as shown.

19 Step fold (see page 5) the top left corner to form the first ear.

20 Repeat step 19 on the right-hand side.

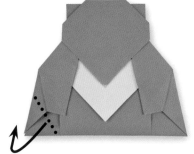

21 Mountain fold back the bottom left corner, as shown.

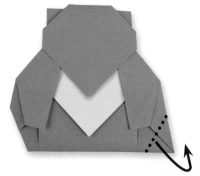

22 Repeat step 21 on the right-hand side.

23 Now you just need to give your raccoon a really cute expression.

Under the Sea

Dive beneath the waves with this collection of amazing underwater creatures.

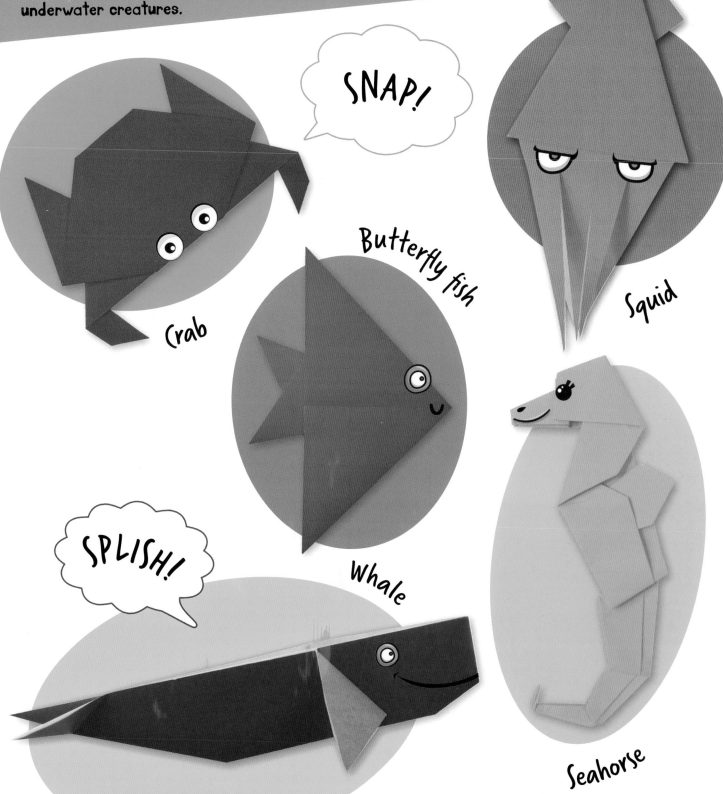

Crab

Butterfly fish

Squid

Whale

Seahorse

Tropical fish

Use these simple steps to fold your own shoal of pretty fish.

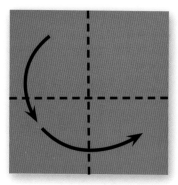

1 Place your paper white side down with a straight edge facing you. Valley fold it in half from top to bottom, and unfold. Then valley fold it in half from left to right, and unfold.

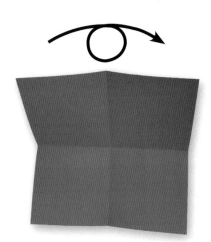

2 Turn the paper over from left to right.

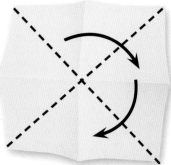

3 Diagonally fold the top left corner to the bottom right, and unfold. Then diagonally fold the top right corner down to the bottom left, and unfold.

Push ▶   ◀ Push

4 Push the two outer edges in to meet each other.

Press

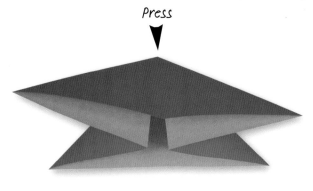

5 Keep pushing and the paper will fold in on itself, forming a triangle shape. Press it down flat.

6 Fold the right point of the top layer over and down, as shown.

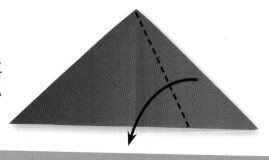

7 Repeat step 6 on the other side, folding the left-hand point over the flap you made in step 6.

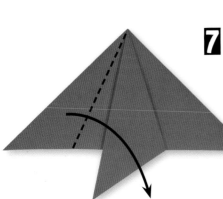

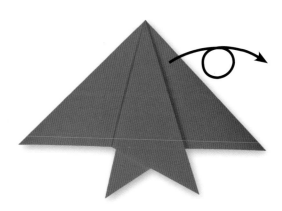

8 Your paper should look like this. Turn it over from left to right.

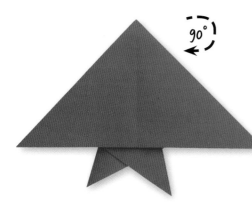

90°

9 Rotate your paper 90° to the right.

10 Give your fish a happy expression. You could add a pattern to its fins and tail, too.

Whale

The blue whale is the largest creature to have ever lived on Earth. It is even bigger than a dinosaur!

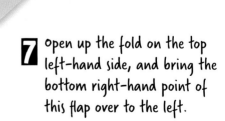

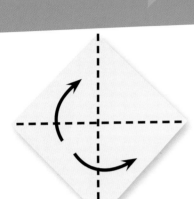

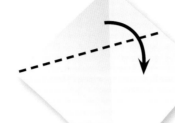

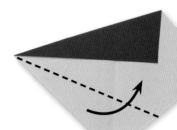

1 Place your paper like this. Fold it in half from left to right, and unfold. Then fold it in half from top to bottom, and unfold.

2 Fold the top corner down to the central crease.

3 Fold the bottom corner up to the central crease.

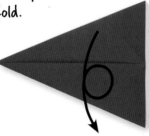

4 Your paper should look like this. Turn it over from top to bottom.

5 Fold the left-hand point all the way over to the right.

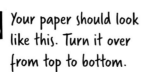

6 Your paper should look like this. Turn it over from top to bottom.

7 Open up the fold on the top left-hand side, and bring the bottom right-hand point of this flap over to the left.

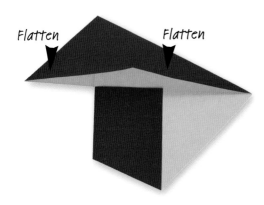

Flatten   Flatten

8 The fold you opened in step 7 should begin to form a triangle shape, like this. Flatten it down.

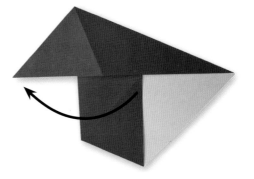

9 Repeat steps 7 and 8 on the other side.

10 Fold the right-hand point of the top layer all the way over to the left.

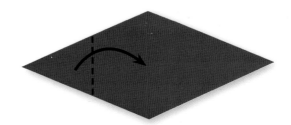

11 Fold the left-hand point to the central crease.

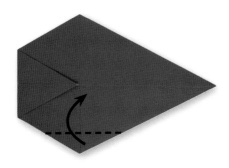

12 Fold the bottom point up, as shown.

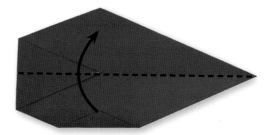

13 Valley fold the paper in half from bottom to top.

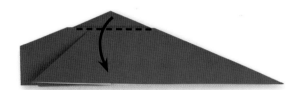

14 Fold the top point down, so it matches the fold you made in step 12. Tuck it inside the paper so it's touching the flap on the opposite side.

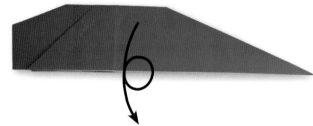

15 Your paper should look like this. Turn it over from top to bottom.

16 Fold the pointed flap down, as shown, to make the first fin.

17 Turn the paper over from left to right and repeat step 16 on the other side.

18 Your paper should look like this. Turn it back again from right to left.

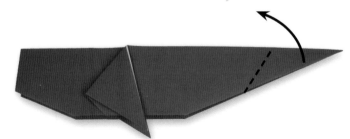

19 To start making the tail, make a valley fold in the right-hand point, as shown, so the point is sticking straight up. Make a strong crease.

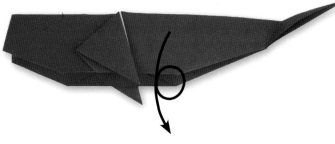

20 Fold it back the other way, so it's also a mountain fold. Again, make sure it's creased well.

21 Turn the paper over from top to bottom, and then open it out so it's lying flat.

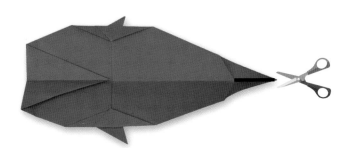

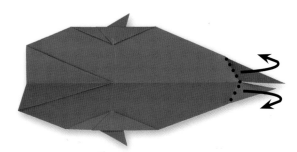

22 Your paper should look like this. Take your scissors and make a small cut up to the point where the folds you made in steps 19 and 20 meet.

23 Mountain fold the folds you made in steps 19 and 20 outward, then close the paper back up.

24

For a final touch, add some eyes, a giant mouth, and, of course, a blowhole on the top of your whale's head.

45

Crab

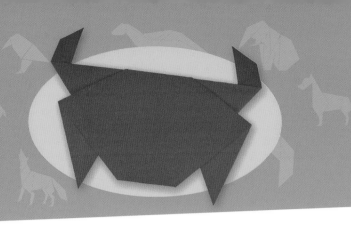

A crab uses its claws to hunt, fight, and attract a mate. Here's how to fold one.

1 Place your paper white side down with a straight edge facing you. Valley fold it in half from top to bottom, and unfold. Then valley fold it in half from left to right, and unfold.

2 Turn the paper over from left to right, so that the white side is facing up.

3 Diagonally fold the top left corner to the bottom right, and unfold. Then diagonally fold the top right corner down to the bottom left, and unfold.

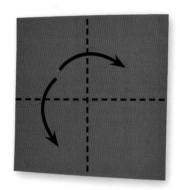

Push   *Push*

4 Push the two outer edges inward to meet each other.

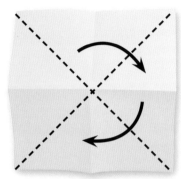

Push

5 Keep pushing and the paper will fold in on itself, forming a triangle shape. Press it down flat.

180°

6 Your paper should look like this. Rotate it 180°, so that the central point is facing you.

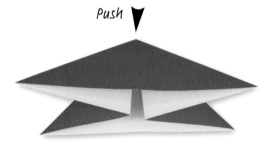

7 Mountain fold the left-hand point of the top layer over and down to form the first claw.

8 Repeat step 7 on the other side to form the other claw.

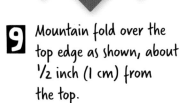

9 Mountain fold over the top edge as shown, about ½ inch (1 cm) from the top.

10 Your paper should look like this. Turn it over from left to right.

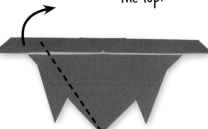

11 Valley fold the left-hand point and edge up, as shown. Aim to get the point facing straight up.

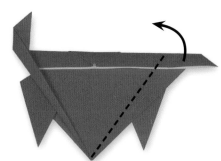

12 Repeat step 11 on the right-hand side.

13 Fold up the bottom point, as shown.

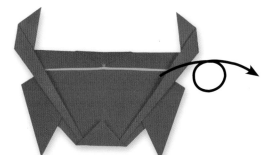

14 Your paper should look like this. Turn it over from left to right.

15 Add some eyes and your crab is ready to scuttle off over the seafloor.

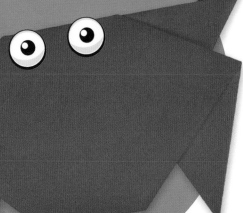

47

Seahorse

A seahorse swims through the water using tiny fins on its back, so make sure you fold them well!

1 Place your paper white side up with a corner facing you. Valley fold it in half from left to right, then unfold.

2 Valley fold the lower left-hand edge so it meets the central crease, as shown.

3 Repeat step 2 on the other side.

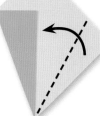

4 Valley fold the upper left edge to the central crease, as shown.

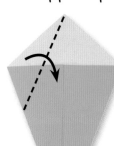

5 Repeat step 4 on the other side.

6 Your paper should look like this.

7 Open out the top left flap. Take hold of the inside flap and pull it down to meet the central crease, making a new flap and crease.

Open

Pull

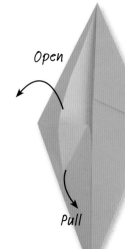

8 Flatten the paper down then repeat step 7 on the other side.

9 Mountain fold the paper in half from right to left.

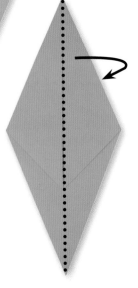

10 Fold up the middle flap so it's pointing to the right.

11 Fold down the tip of the right-hand point, so it's now pointing straight down.

12 Fold the tip the other way so it's also a mountain fold.

13 Open up the fold a little and tuck the tip inside to make an inside reverse fold (see page 6).

Tuck

14 Your paper should look like this. Turn it over from right to left and repeat steps 10 to 13 on the other side.

15 Turn it back again from left to right, then fold the left point of the top layer over to the right, as shown.

16 Turn the paper over from left to right and repeat step 15 on the other side, so the two sides match. Then turn the paper back over again from right to left.

17 Valley fold the top point over to the right.

18 Fold it the other way so it's also a mountain fold.

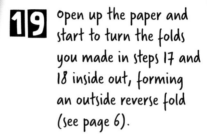

19 Open up the paper and start to turn the folds you made in steps 17 and 18 inside out, forming an outside reverse fold (see page 6).

20 Valley fold the top right-hand point back to the left.

21 Fold it the other way so it's also a mountain fold.

22 Again, open up the paper and start to turn the folds you made in steps 20 and 21 inside out to form an outside reverse fold.

23 Make a step fold (see page 5), as shown.

Tuck

25 Tuck the folds you made in steps 23 and 24 inside each other.

24 Your paper should look like this. Crease both folds in the step fold back the other way.

Tuck ▶

26 Fold the top left point back to the right, as shown.

27 Fold it back the other way, so it's also a mountain fold. Make sure it's creased well.

28 Turn the folds you made in steps 26 and 27 into an inside reverse fold to form the nose.

29 Make an angled step fold about halfway down the body, as shown, to form the tail.

30 Make another angled step farther down the tail, as shown.

33 Seahorses like to swim in pairs. Why not fold yours a friend to keep her company?

31 Make a final step fold in the tail.

32 Valley fold the end of the tail up.

Squid

Giant squid can be as long as a school bus!
Here's how to fold a paper version.

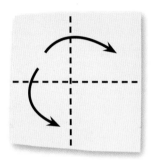

1 Place your paper like this. Fold it in half from left to right, and unfold. Then fold it in half from top to bottom, and unfold.

2 Rotate the paper 45° to the right, so that a corner is facing you.

3 Fold the paper in half from top to bottom, then unfold.

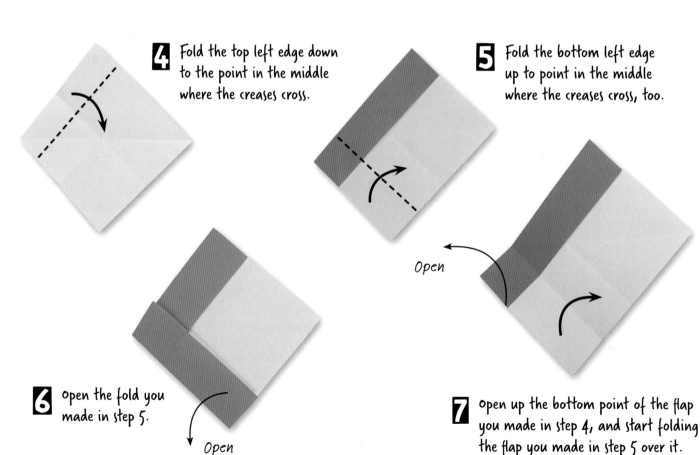

4 Fold the top left edge down to the point in the middle where the creases cross.

5 Fold the bottom left edge up to point in the middle where the creases cross, too.

Open

6 Open the fold you made in step 5.

Open

7 Open up the bottom point of the flap you made in step 4, and start folding the flap you made in step 5 over it.

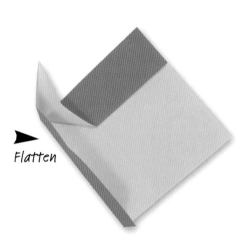

Flatten

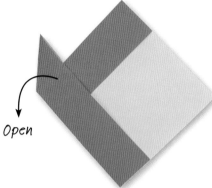

Open

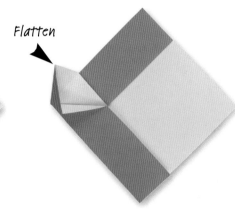

Flatten

8 Your paper should begin to look like this. Flatten it down.

9 Unfold the flap you've just made slightly.

10 Separate the top and bottom layers of the flap and pull them apart till they form a shape like a bird's mouth, like this, then flatten the shape down.

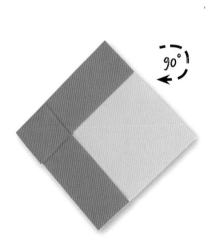

90°

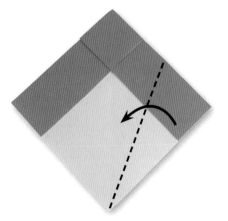

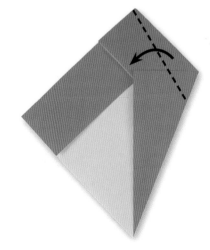

12 Fold the lower right edge over to the central line, as shown.

11 Your paper should look this. Rotate it 90° to the right, so the shape you made in step 10 is at the top and a corner is facing you.

13 Fold the upper right edge over to the central line, tucking it under the shape you made in step 10.

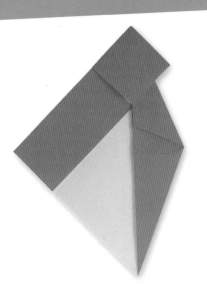

14 Your paper should look like this. Repeat steps 12 and 13 on the left-hand side.

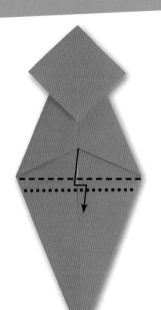

15 Make a step fold, as shown (see page 5).

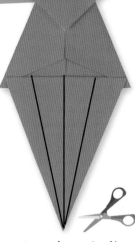

16 Use scissors to make three straight cuts up to the horizontal fold line, as shown.

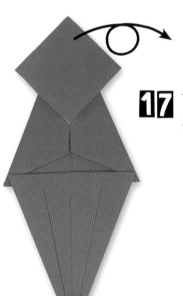

17 Turn the paper over from left to right.

18 Fan the tentacles out to get your squid prepared for its first swim. Remember, when adding features, that squid have very large eyes.

In the Jungle

Use these cute models to make your own spectacular jungle scene.

Parrot

Tiger

GROWL!

Gorilla

Crocodile

SNAP!

Crocodile

Follow these steps to fold a fierce crocodile.
Make sure you draw on some sharp teeth!

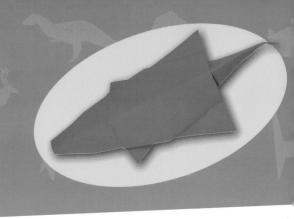

1 Place your paper like this with the white side up and a corner facing you. Make a valley fold from left to right, then unfold.

2 Valley fold the left corner to meet the middle crease.

3 Valley fold the right corner to the middle crease, too.

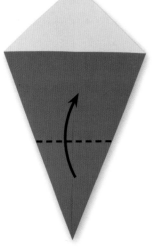

4 Valley fold the bottom point up, so the point sits just above the flaps formed in steps 2 and 3.

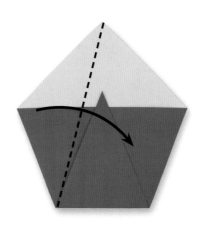

5 Valley fold the left-hand point across and down.

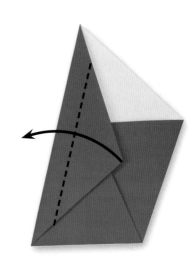

6 Now valley fold the point back to the left again.

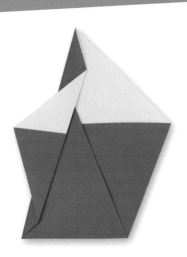

7 Your paper should look like this. Repeat steps 5 and 6 on the right-hand side.

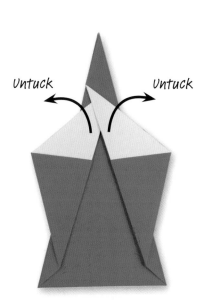

Untuck   Untuck

8 Untuck the point you made in step 4.

9 Bring the middle point down to the bottom.

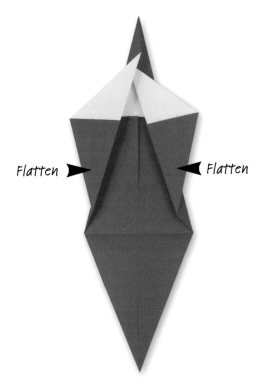

Flatten ▶   ◀ Flatten

10 Your paper should look like this. Flatten down the side folds again.

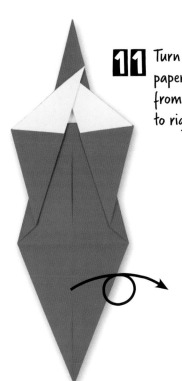

11 Turn your paper over from left to right.

180°

12 Now rotate your paper 180°.

57

Crocodile... continued

13 Make a valley fold just above the central fold.

Push

14 Push the valley fold you made in step 13 behind the central fold to form a step fold (see page 5).

15 Form the tail by making a step fold at the other end. The mountain fold should line up with the lower points on the left and right side.

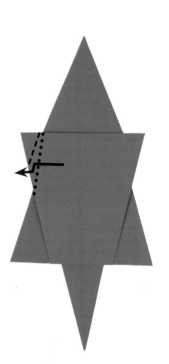

16 Make a step fold at a slight angle in the top-left corner. This is a foot.

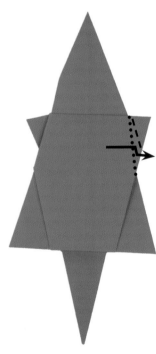

17 Repeat step 16 on the other side.

18 Make a small mountain fold at the top to form the snout.

19 Push the sides together slightly along the middle crease. This will give your crocodile a 3-D shape.

Push ► ◄ Push

20 Push the ends of the tail together, and curl them to one side.

Push ►◄ Push

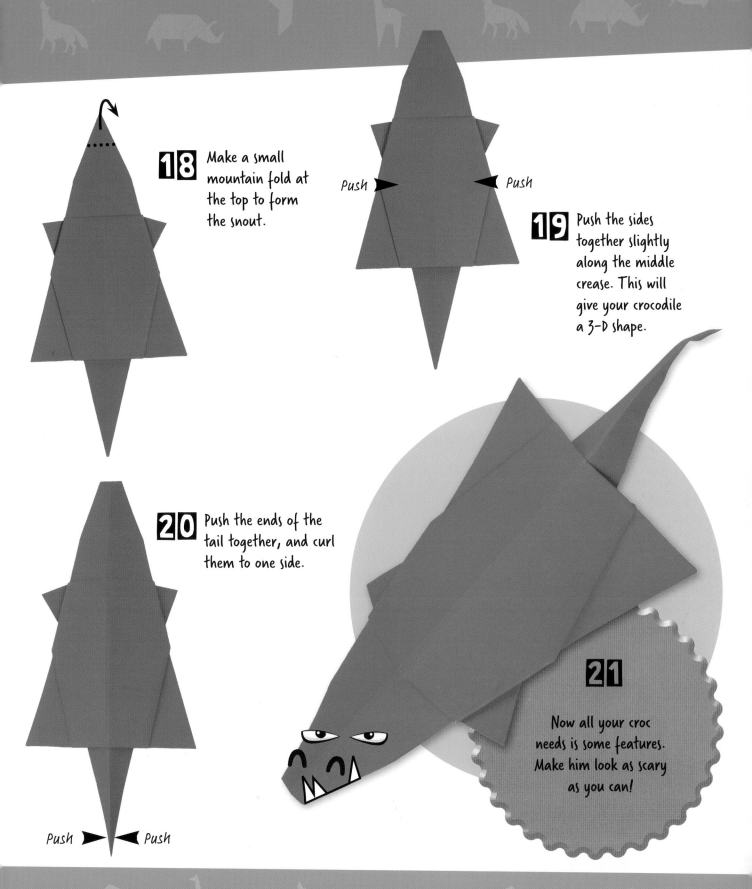

21 Now all your croc needs is some features. Make him look as scary as you can!

Gorilla

Gorillas are the world's largest apes. Follow these steps to fold your own gentle giant.

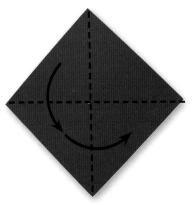

1 Place your paper white side down with a corner facing you. Valley fold it in half from top to bottom, and unfold. Then valley fold it in half from left to right, and unfold.

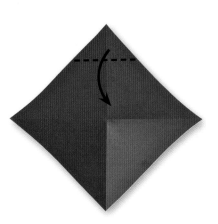

2 Fold the top tip down to the middle of the paper where the creases cross.

3 Make a small valley fold, as shown.

4 Turn the paper over from left to right.

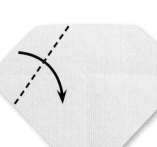

5 Fold the top left edge in so it is about ¼ inch (5 mm) from the central crease, as shown.

6 Repeat step 5 on the right-hand side.

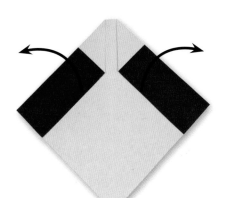

7 Unfold the folds you made in steps 5 and 6.

8 Make a small diagonal valley fold on the left-hand side, as shown.

9 Repeat step 8 on the right-hand side.

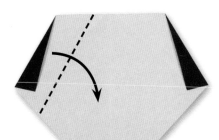

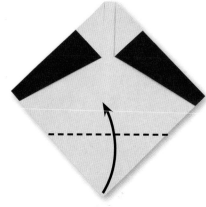

10 Refold the fold you made in step 5 over the fold you made in step 8.

11 Repeat step 10 on the right-hand side.

12 Fold up the bottom point, as shown. It should touch the point where the horizontal and vertical creases cross.

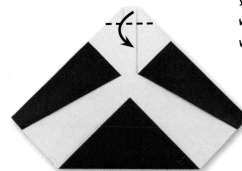

13 Make a small fold at the top of the paper.

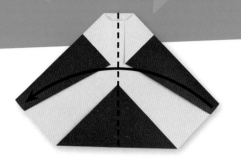

14 Fold the paper in half from right to left.

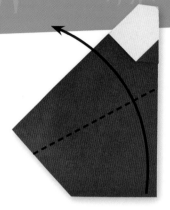

15 Fold up the bottom edge, as shown.

Unfold

16 Unfold the fold you made in step 15.

17 Rotate the paper 90° to the left, so the white area is on the left-hand side.

90°

Push

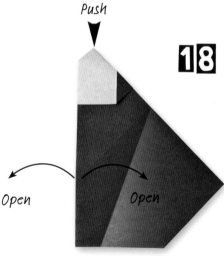

Open

Open

18 Open up the flaps on the left-hand side. As you do, push down the top point.

Flatten

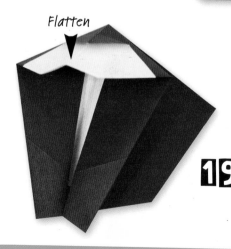

19 Your paper should look like this. Flatten the white area down to make the face.

20 Mountain fold the left-hand corner behind.

Tuck

21 Fold it the other way, so it's also a valley fold.

22 Tuck the fold inside to make an inside reverse fold (see page 6).

23 Your paper should look like this. Repeat steps 20 to 22 on the other side of the face.

Unfold

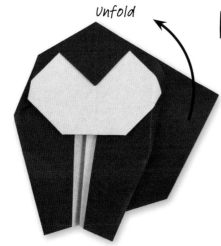

24 Unfold the body and your gorilla should stand up.

25

Use your pens to draw your gorilla's face. Will he be fierce or friendly?

Tiger

A tiger's stripes helps it to blend into the forest. Here's how to fold your own stealthy hunter.

1 Place your paper white side up with a corner facing you. Valley fold it in half from left to right, and unfold.

2 Fold the top right edge over to the central crease.

3 Repeat step 2 on the left-hand side.

4 Make a small fold along the bottom right edge, as shown.

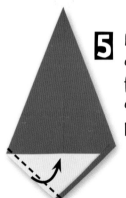 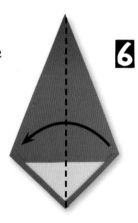 

5 Repeat step 4 on the other side. The new flap will go over the one created in the previous step.

6 Fold the paper in half from right to left.

7 Your paper should look like this. Rotate it about 45° to the left so the bottom left edge is facing you.

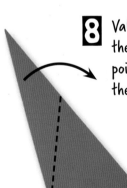 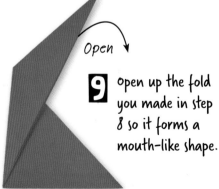 

8 Valley fold the top left point over to the right.

Open

9 Open up the fold you made in step 8 so it forms a mouth-like shape.

Push

10 As you open up the fold, push down the top point.

64

Flatten   Flatten

11 Your paper should form a triangle shape. Flatten it down.

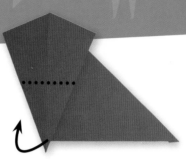

12 Mountain fold the bottom point up to form the face.

13 Make a step fold (see page 5), as shown, to form the first ear.

14 Repeat step 13 on the other side.

15 Make the tail by valley folding the right point back to the left. Fold it the other way so it's also a mountain fold.

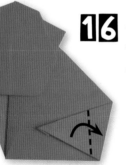

16 Make another valley fold, slightly further to the right, as shown. Again, fold it the other way so it's also a mountain fold.

17 Turn the folds made in steps 15 and 16 into two inside reverse folds (see page 6), one inside the other.

18 Add some eyes, a nose, whiskers, and, of course, stripes. Your paper tiger is all set to go prowling through the jungle.

Parrot

Parrots have beautiful, bright feathers. Choose a tropical shade of paper for yours!

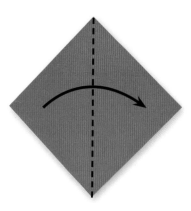

1 Place your paper white side down with a corner facing you. Valley fold it in half from left to right, and unfold.

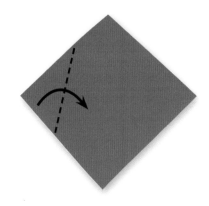

2 Fold the left corner in, so the tip meets the central crease, as shown.

3 Repeat step 2 on the right-hand side.

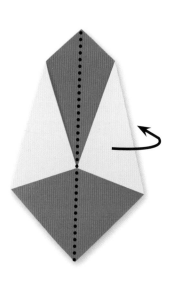

4 Mountain fold the paper in half, so the vertical crease is on the right.

5 Your paper should look like this. Fold the top point over to the left.

6 Fold it back the other way so it's also a mountain fold.

Tuck

7 Tuck the fold in on itself to form an inside reverse fold (see page 6).

8 Fold the top left point down.

9 Fold it back the other way so it's also a mountain fold.

Tuck

10 Tuck the fold over to make an outside reverse fold (see page 6).

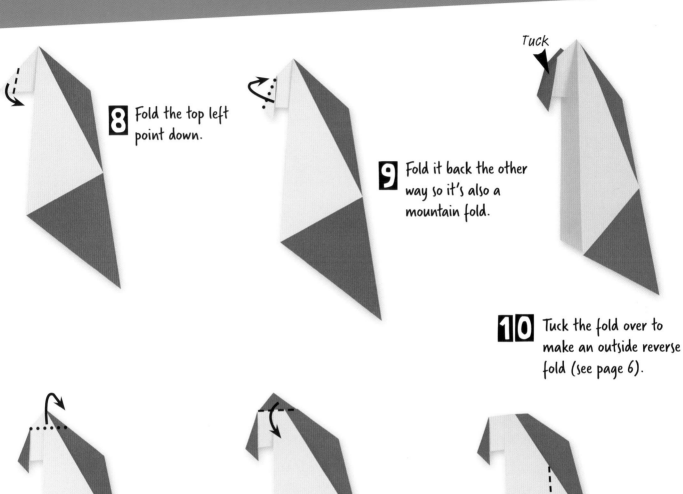

11 Mountain fold over the top point of the top layer, and tuck it into the middle of your paper.

12 Your paper should look like this. Now valley fold the top point of the bottom layer and tuck it into the middle of your paper.

13 Make the first wing by folding the white point to the left edge.

Parrot... continued

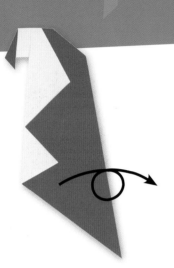

14 Your paper should look like this. Turn it over from left to right.

15 Repeat step 13 on this side, then turn the paper back from right to left.

16 Use a pair of scissors to make a cut in the bottom of the paper, as shown.

17 Valley fold the top layer over to the left to make the first foot.

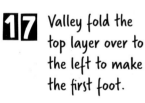

18 Do the same on the bottom layer to make the other foot.

19 Spread the feet out and your parrot should be able to stand up.

In the Desert

All of the animals in this chapter like it hot! Here's how to fold your own collection of desert creatures.

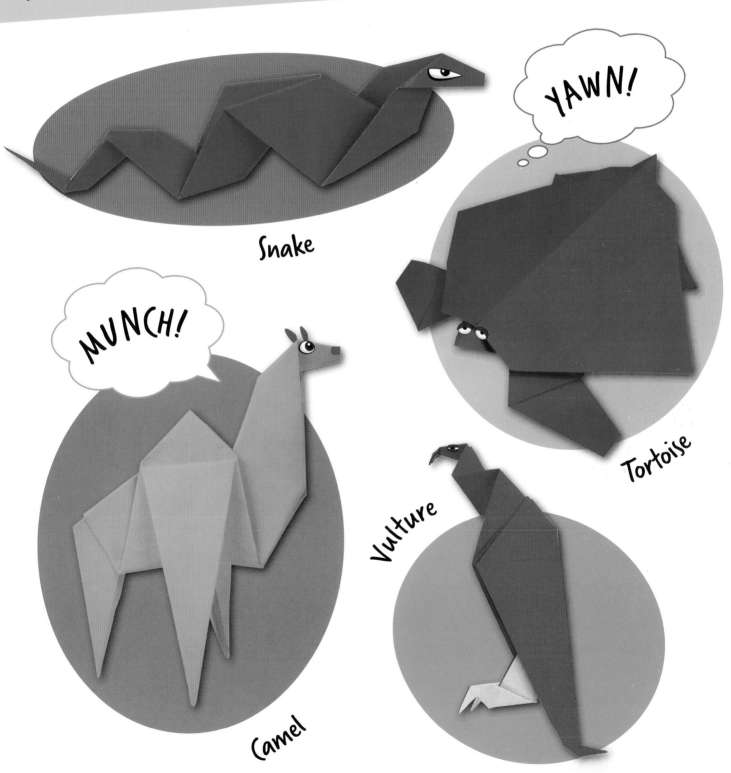

Snake

YAWN!

Tortoise

MUNCH!

Camel

Vulture

Camel

Follow the instructions to make your own one-humped camel, also known as a "dromedary".

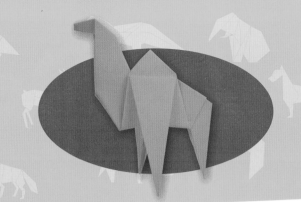

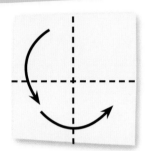

1 Place your paper white side up with a straight edge facing you. Valley fold it in half from top to bottom, and unfold. Then valley fold it in half from left to right, and unfold.

2 Turn the paper over, so that the white side is now facing down. Diagonally valley fold it one way and unfold. Then diagonally valley fold it the other way and unfold.

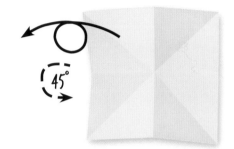

3 Turn the paper over again, so the white side is facing up. Rotate it 45° so a corner is facing you.

Push   Push

4 Start pushing the two outer corners in toward each other.

Flatten

5 As you push, the paper should start folding up into a small square like this. Flatten it down.

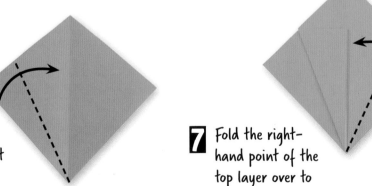

6 Fold the left-hand point of the top layer over to the central crease.

7 Fold the right-hand point of the top layer over to the central crease.

70

Hard

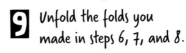

8 Fold the top point down, as shown.

9 Unfold the folds you made in steps 6, 7, and 8.

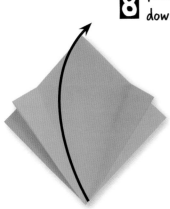

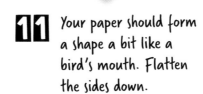

Flatten ▶   ◀ Flatten

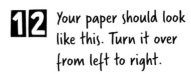

10 Lift the bottom point of the top layer up to the top.

11 Your paper should form a shape a bit like a bird's mouth. Flatten the sides down.

12 Your paper should look like this. Turn it over from left to right.

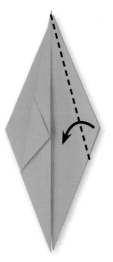

13 Now, repeat steps 6 to 11 on this side of the model.

14 Your paper should now look like this. Fold the left-hand point of the top layer over to the central crease.

15 Repeat step 14 on the other side.

71

Camel... continued

16 Your paper should look like this. Turn it over from left to right.

17 Fold the left-hand point over to the central crease.

18 Fold the right-hand point over to the central crease.

19 Valley fold the bottom left point up and to the left, as shown.

20 Fold it the other way so it's also a mountain fold.

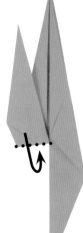

21 Open up the fold and tuck it in to form an inside reverse fold (see page 6). *Tuck*

22 Your paper should look like this. Repeat steps 19 to 21 on the other side.

23 Valley fold the right-hand point down, and then back the other way so it's also a mountain fold.

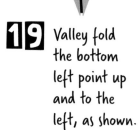

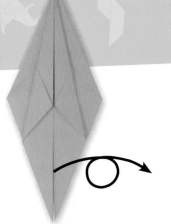

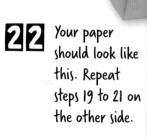

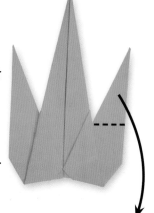

Tuck

24 Open up the fold and tuck it in to form an inside reverse fold.

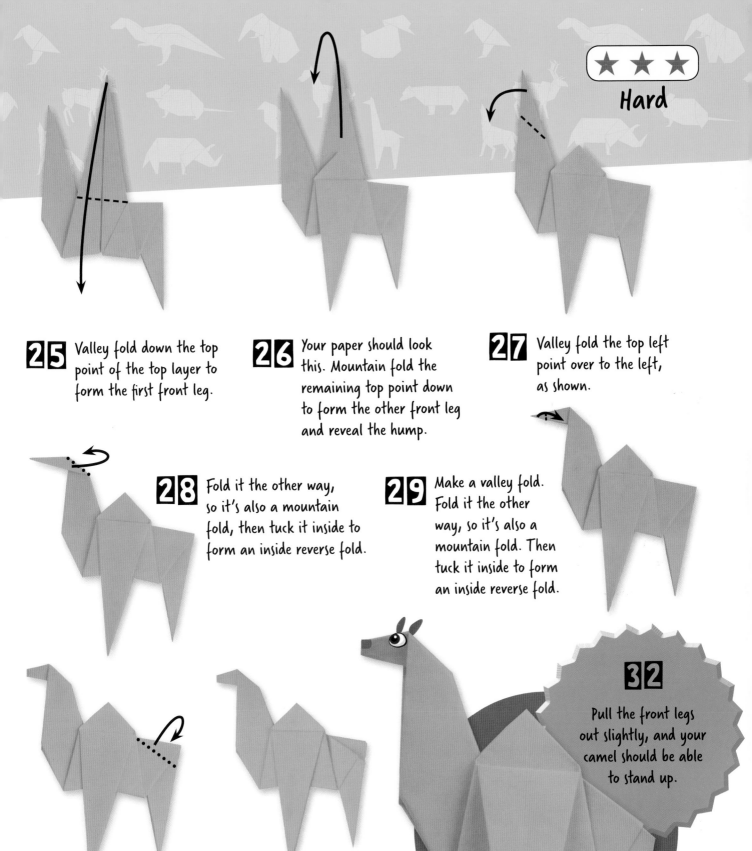

25 Valley fold down the top point of the top layer to form the first front leg.

26 Your paper should look this. Mountain fold the remaining top point down to form the other front leg and reveal the hump.

27 Valley fold the top left point over to the left, as shown.

28 Fold it the other way, so it's also a mountain fold, then tuck it inside to form an inside reverse fold.

29 Make a valley fold. Fold it the other way, so it's also a mountain fold. Then tuck it inside to form an inside reverse fold.

30 Mountain fold the top layer of the right corner, and tuck the flap inside the paper.

31 Your paper should look like this. Repeat step 30 on the other side.

32 Pull the front legs out slightly, and your camel should be able to stand up.

73

Snake

Snakes are cold-blooded, so they warm themselves up by lying in the sun.

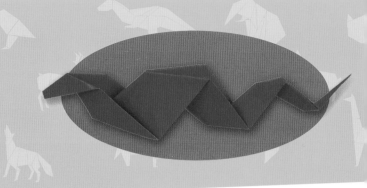

1 Place your paper like this with the white side up and corner facing you. Make a valley fold from left to right, then unfold.

2 Fold the left corner to the central crease.

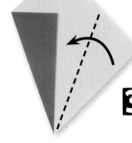

3 Fold the right corner to the central crease.

4 Again, fold the left corner to the middle.

5 Repeat step 4 on the right-hand side.

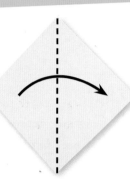

6 Make a valley fold, as shown, on the top left-hand side of the paper. It should also meet the central line.

7 Repeat step 6 on the right-hand side.

90°

8 Your paper should look like this. Turn it over from left to right, and then rotate it 90° to the left.

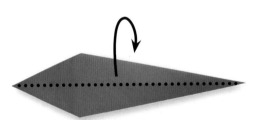

9 Mountain fold the paper in half from top to bottom. Rotate it to the right so the straight edge is facing you.

74

10 Make a valley fold, like this. Fold it the other way to make a mountain fold. Then turn it into outside reverse fold (see page 6).

11 Make a valley fold slightly farther down the paper. Fold it the other way, so it's also a mountain fold, then fold it in on itself.

12 Your paper should be loose, rather than flat, like this. Repeat step 11 four more times further along the paper, in the positions marked.

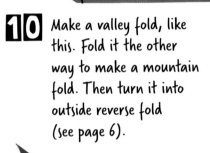

13 Your paper should look like this. Make a valley fold at the left-hand end, as shown.

14 Fold it back the other way so it's also a mountain fold. Then fold it over itself to form an outside reverse fold.

15 Make a small valley fold at the left-hand end, as shown.

Tuck

16 Fold it back the other way so it's also a mountain fold. Then tuck it in to form an inside reverse fold (see page 6).

17

Add some eyes and your snake is ready to slither off across the sand.

Tortoise

Desert tortoises hardly ever need to drink. They get their water from food, instead.

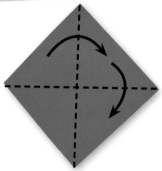

1 Place your paper white side down with a corner facing you. Valley fold it in half from top to bottom, and unfold. Then valley fold it in half from left to right, and unfold.

2 Turn the paper over, so that the white side is now facing up. Diagonally fold it one way, and unfold. Then diagonally valley fold it the other way, and unfold.

Push

Push

3 Start pushing the two outer corners in toward each other.

Flatten

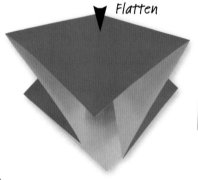

4 As you push, the paper should start folding up into a small square like this. Flatten it down.

5 Fold the left-hand point of the top layer over to the central crease.

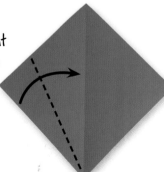

6 Fold the right-hand point of the top layer over to the central crease.

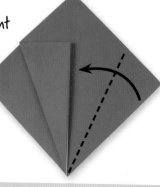

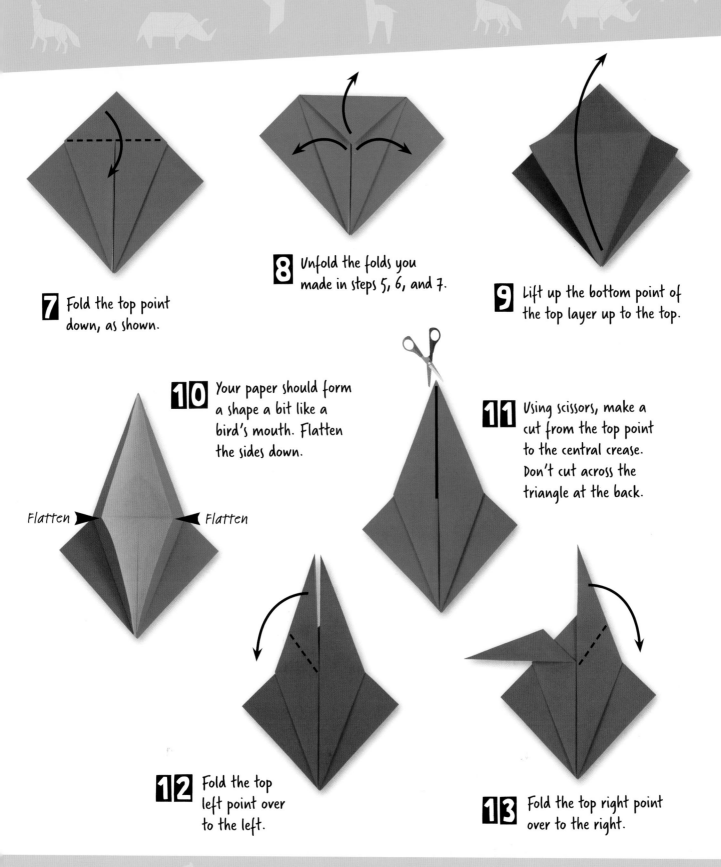

7 Fold the top point down, as shown.

8 Unfold the folds you made in steps 5, 6, and 7.

9 Lift up the bottom point of the top layer up to the top.

10 Your paper should form a shape a bit like a bird's mouth. Flatten the sides down.

Flatten ▶   ◀ Flatten

11 Using scissors, make a cut from the top point to the central crease. Don't cut across the triangle at the back.

12 Fold the top left point over to the left.

13 Fold the top right point over to the right.

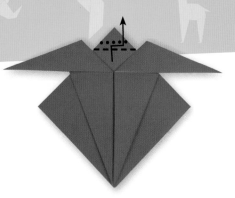

14 Make a step fold at the top, as shown.

15 Your paper should look like this. Fold the top left-hand point to the right.

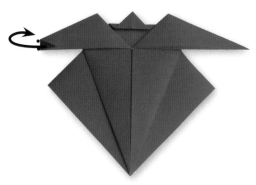

16 Fold it the other way, so it's also a mountain fold.

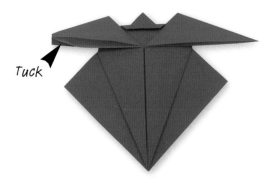

Tuck

17 Open up the fold and tuck it in to form an inside reverse fold (see page 6).

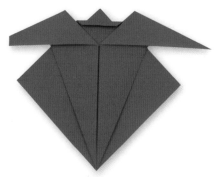

18 Your paper should look like this. Repeat steps 15 to 17 on the right-hand side.

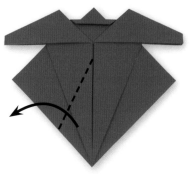

19 Fold the bottom left point across to the left, as shown.

20 Your paper should look like this. Repeat step 19 on the other side.

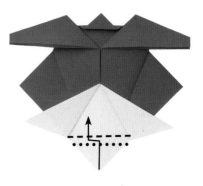

21 Make a step fold at the bottom, as shown.

22 Your paper should look like this. Turn it over from left to right.

23

Slightly fold the shell and point the legs down. Your tortoise should be able to stand and walk (very slowly, of course).

Vulture

Vultures have excellent senses of sight and smell, which help them find food.

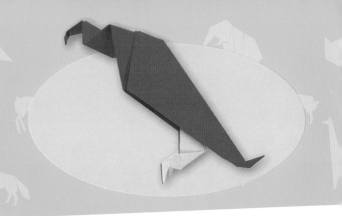

1 Place your paper white side up with a straight edge facing you. Valley fold it in half from top to bottom, and unfold. Then valley fold it in half from left to right, and unfold.

2 Turn the paper over, so that the white side is now facing down. Diagonally valley fold it one way and unfold. Then diagonally valley fold it the other way and unfold.

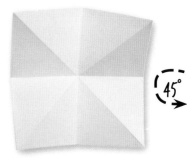

3 Turn the paper over again, so the white side is facing up. Rotate it 45° so a corner is facing you.

Push   Push

4 Start pushing the two outer corners in toward each other.

Flatten

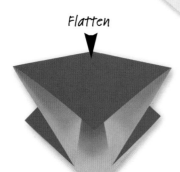

5 As you push, the paper should start folding up into a small square like this. Flatten it down.

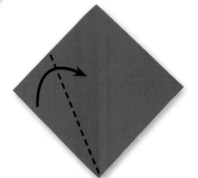

6 Now fold the left-hand point of the top layer over to the central crease.

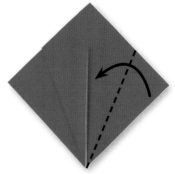

7 Fold the right-hand point of the top layer over to the central crease.

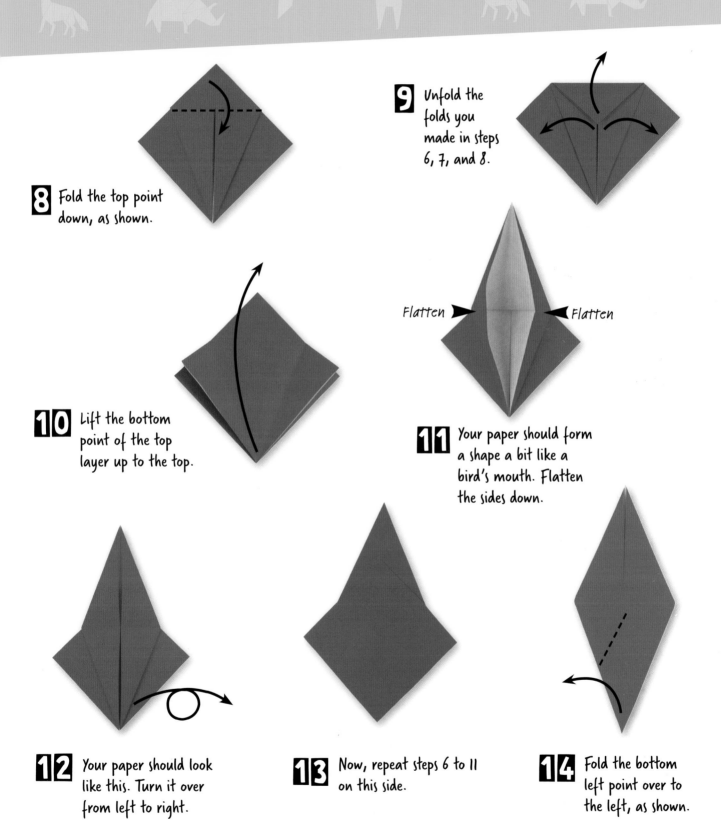

9 Unfold the folds you made in steps 6, 7, and 8.

8 Fold the top point down, as shown.

10 Lift the bottom point of the top layer up to the top.

Flatten ► ◄ Flatten

11 Your paper should form a shape a bit like a bird's mouth. Flatten the sides down.

12 Your paper should look like this. Turn it over from left to right.

13 Now, repeat steps 6 to 11 on this side.

14 Fold the bottom left point over to the left, as shown.

Vulture... continued

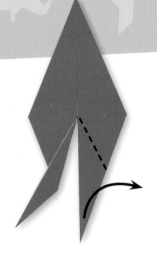

15 Repeat step 14 on the right-hand side.

Turn over

16 Turn the fold you made in step 14 over on itself to form an outside reverse fold (see page 6).

17 Your paper should look like this. Repeat step 16 on the right-hand side.

18 Bring the top point of the back layer down to the bottom.

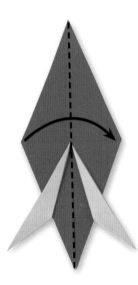

19 Valley fold your paper in half from left to right.

20 Rotate your paper slightly to the right.

21 Fold the bottom point over to the right.

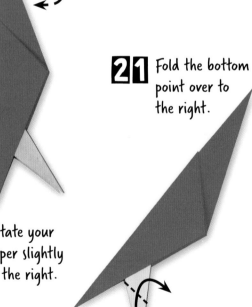

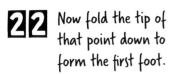

22 Now fold the tip of that point down to form the first foot.

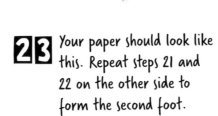

23 Your paper should look like this. Repeat steps 21 and 22 on the other side to form the second foot.

24 Mountain fold the top point over and to the right, as shown.

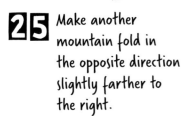

25 Make another mountain fold in the opposite direction slightly farther to the right.

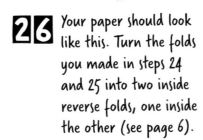

26 Your paper should look like this. Turn the folds you made in steps 24 and 25 into two inside reverse folds, one inside the other (see page 6).

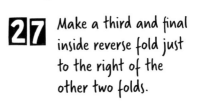

27 Make a third and final inside reverse fold just to the right of the other two folds.

28 Fold down the right point to make the end of the beak.

29 Fold the bottom left point up, as shown.

30 Turn the fold into an outside reverse fold to form the tail.

31

Pull out the tail and feet, and your vulture should be able stand up. He's on the look out for his next meal!

On the Ice

Learn how to fold a super-cool cast of Arctic and Antarctic animals in this chapter.

SPLISH!

Narwhal

Arctic hare

Penguin

BRRR!

Polar bear

Arctic hare

In winter, this hare's fur turns bright white to
help hide it against the snow.

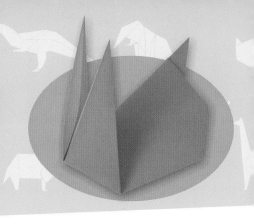

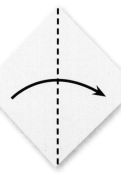

1 Place your paper white side up
with a corner facing you. Valley
fold it in half from left to
right, then unfold.

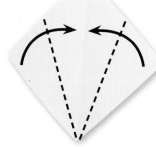

2 Fold the left and right points
to the central crease.

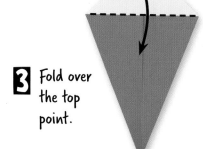

3 Fold over
the top
point.

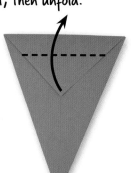

4 Fold the point back up
again so it just reaches over
the top of the paper.

5 Make two small valley
folds on the left and
right sides.

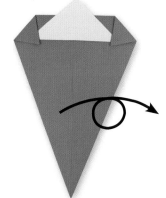

6 Your paper should look
like this. Turn it over
from left to right.

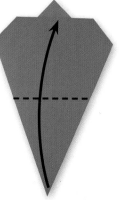

7 Fold the bottom
point up to the
top edge.

8 Unfold and turn the
paper 90° to the right.

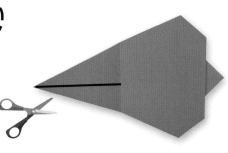

9 Use scissors to cut from
the left point to the
vertical crease.

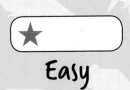

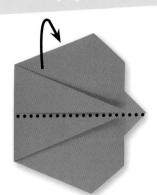

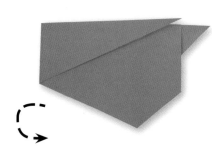

10 Fold the left points over to the right.

11 Mountain fold the paper in half from top to bottom.

12 Your paper should look like this. Rotate it slightly to the left, so the straight edge is facing you.

Pull

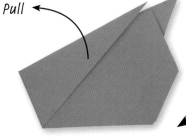

13 Pull the first ear up.

Crease

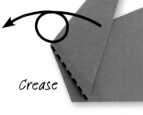

14 Crease well along the line shown. Then turn the paper over from right to left.

16

Once the ears are lined up, open them out so your hare can listen out for danger. What other origami animals do you think she can hear?

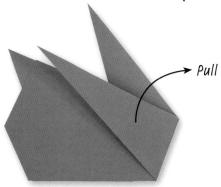

Pull

15 Repeat steps 13 and 14 on this side.

Penguin

Penguins are excellent swimmers, zipping
through the icy waters on the hunt for food.

1 Place your paper like this.
Valley fold it in half from left
to right, then unfold.

2 Valley fold the left corner,
then valley fold the right
corner, as shown.

3 Make two small valley
folds in the flaps you
created in step 2.

 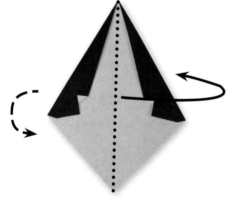 

6 Valley fold the top
left point over to
the right, as shown.

4 Make two small valley
folds, as shown.

5 Mountain fold in half from
right to left, and rotate
the paper slightly so a
straight edge is facing you.

9 Your paper will
look like this.
Unfold the fold
you just made
and then make
a smaller fold
back to the left.

8 Fold the right-
hand point back
to the left.

7 Fold it the other way so it's a
mountain fold. Turn this into an
outside reverse fold (see page 6).

10 Your paper will look like this. Unfold the second fold, too.

11 Turn the folds you made in steps 9 and 10 into two inside reverse folds (see page 6), one inside the other.

◄ Tuck

12 Flatten your paper down, and then make a small valley fold in the bottom right, as shown.

13 Your paper should look like this. Repeat step 12 on the other side, and then turn both folds into inside reverse folds.

14 Fold the top right-hand point down to the left, as shown.

15 Now make another small fold back to the right.

16 Turn the folds you made in steps 14 and 15 into two inside reverse folds, one inside the other.

17
Your penguin is complete. Why not make her some friends?

Polar bear

These enormous bears are the world's largest land predators. And they can swim well too!

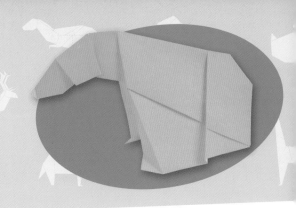

1 Place your paper white side up with a corner facing you. Valley fold it in half from right to left, then unfold.

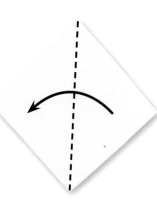

2 Make two valley folds on either side, as shown, then unfold.

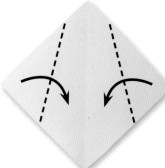

3 Fold the left side back in.

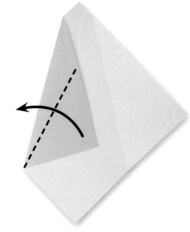

4 Make a small valley fold on the left-hand side, as shown.

5 Your paper should look like this. Repeat steps 3 and 4 on the right-hand side.

6 Fold the bottom point up.

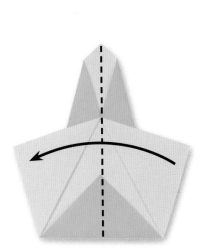

7 Valley fold the paper in half from right to left.

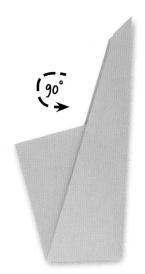

8 Your paper should look like this. Rotate the paper 90° to the left, so the shorter, straight edge is facing you.

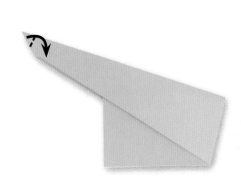

9 Make a valley fold near the left point. Fold it the other way so it's also a mountain fold, then turn it into an outside reverse fold (see page 6).

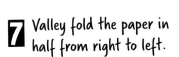

10 Make an angled step fold, as shown (see page 5).

11 Make another angled step fold, slightly farther to the right.

12 Turn the folds you made in steps 10 and 11 into two inside reverse folds (see page 6), tucking them one inside the other.

13 Your paper should look like this. Open up the fold you made in step 7, so the paper is lying flat.

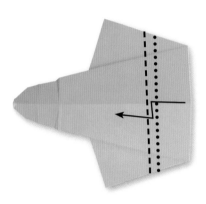

14 Make a step fold on the right-hand side.

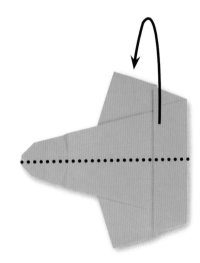

15 Refold the paper in half from top to bottom.

16 Make a small valley fold on the right-hand side.

17 Fold it the other way so it's also a mountain fold.

18 Tuck the fold in to form an inside reverse fold.

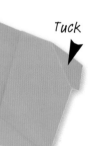

Tuck

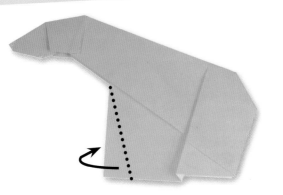

19 Make a mountain fold in the top layer of paper to form the first front leg.

20 Make a small valley fold to form a foot.

21 Your paper should look like this. Repeat steps 19 and 20 on the other side to make the other leg and foot.

22

It's time for your polar bear to start prowling across the Arctic tundra.

Narwhal

Sometimes called "sea unicorns", these whales have an enormous tusk on the front of their heads.

1 Place your paper white side up with a corner facing you. Valley fold it in half from left to right, then unfold.

2 Valley fold the right corner to the central crease, as shown.

3 Repeat step 2 on the other side.

4 Valley fold the upper left edge to the central crease, as shown.

Open ←

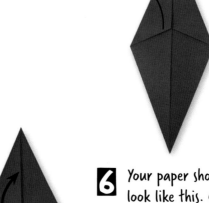

5 Repeat step 4 on the other side.

6 Your paper should look like this. Open out the top left flap.

Pull

7 Take hold of the top of the inside flap and pull it down, but don't flatten it.

8 Instead, fold the flap back and up to the top, to make a new flap.

9 Flatten the paper down, then repeat steps 7 and 8 on the other side.

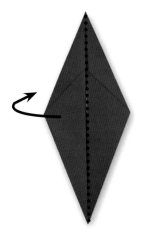

10 Your paper should look like this. Mountain fold it in half from left to right.

11 Fold the middle point down and over to the left, as shown.

12 Turn your paper over from left to right.

13 Fold the second middle point down and over to the right, as shown.

14 Your paper should look like this. Fold the bottom point over to the left, as shown.

15 Fold it the other way, so it's also a mountain fold. Then turn it into an inside reverse fold (see page 6).

16 Fold the top point down, as shown.

17 Fold it back up again to form a step fold (see page 5).

95

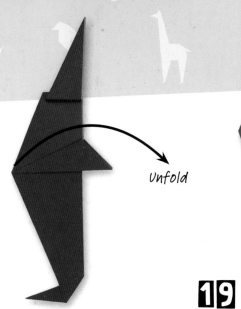

18 Unfold the paper from left to right and flatten down the step fold made in steps 16 and 17.

Unfold

19 Your paper should look like this. Make a small valley fold in the top left-hand edge, as shown. Crease it down well.

20 Repeat step 19 on the other side.

21 Fold the paper back together again, being sure to keep the step folds you made in steps 19 and 20 in place.

22

With its all-important tusk now in place, your narwhal is ready to join his friends.